Nice Guys
Finish First

Jard DeVille

NICE GUYS
FINISH FIRST

How to Get People
to Do What You Want
... and Thank You for It

William Morrow and Company, Inc.
New York   1979

Library of Congress Cataloging in Publication Data

DeVille, Jard.
    Nice guys finish first.

    Bibliography: p.
    1. Success.   2. Influence (Psychology)   I. Title.
BF637.S8D43   158'.1   79-637
ISBN 0-688-03471-3

Printed in the United States of America.

First Edition

1 2 3 4 5 6 7 8 9 10

*To Roberta, who has made it all
possible by never losing the faith*

Acknowledgments

I am deeply indebted to my students at various colleges and in many seminars. They continually pressed for better ways of relating and of persuading others, ways that were more effective than conventional wisdom about interpersonal leadership in business, education, family, and the church. They pushed me beyond psychological orthodoxy to a better way. I thank them once more for sharing their dreams, shortcomings, and strategies with me.

Contents

Introduction

This book is about people and about winning and losing in life, since winning and losing are the only options that are open. It is written with the knowledge that neither power nor pleasure exists in a vacuum. Virtually everything you do in life involves other people in some way. Therefore, you will have to overpower, outskill, deceive, or persuade certain of them before they will allow you to share in the marbles, money, stimulating partners, or promotions you want. And few of the people who are winning are willing to share their hard-earned knowledge with you.

The purpose of this book is to teach you how to predict the attitudes and actions of the men and women you must influence every day. It also shows you how to influence their choices in ways they approve by using new methods of interpersonal effectiveness. You can do these things by learning and using powerful new techniques developed by psychiatrists and psychologists. These methods are unknown to most people, although professional therapists have been using them for decades with great success.

Most people struggle through life the best way they can, winning once in a while, but more often losing, because they never learned how to make things happen for them.

They try to win by using the attitudes, expectations, and skills they chanced to learn in childhood. Unfortunately, in this age of relentless change, when power and authority are shared by more and more people, to have to depend on what you picked up in childhood is a poor way to shape your life into a winning affair.

In the last quarter of the twentieth century, life has become too complex to be left to traditional behavioral patterns that have been handed down from generation to generation. At home you were probably conditioned not to ask embarrassing questions. At school you were expected to memorize the correct answers. If you are like most people, you are still waiting for someone to ask the right questions so you can show what a good student you were. No one is ever going to ask them, since most of the answers you learned are no longer appropriate. Yet millions of men and women who would never think of crossing the country by train instead of aircraft, who would never take some medicine man's snake-oil cure, try to win with people by using methods that were outdated half a century ago. And they cannot understand why they aren't among the winners in life.

Today, men and women are having to cope with events that are affecting their lives in many crucial ways. Medicine, interpersonal behavior, education, sexual mores, and business are all changing more rapidly than at any time in history. None of the changes has such critical implications as the attitude that people have toward power and control. The John Wayne mystique doesn't impress anyone anymore. Almost everyone is developing a better sense of his own independence.

Not long ago a middle-aged businessman told of an experience he had with his secretary. He said that the young woman was a hardworking, high-spirited employee who was competent and loyal enough to become his assistant. But he began to notice, to his displeasure, that she was dressing more and more casually, as if she were going to a picnic rather than to business. So he called her into his office and tactfully asked her to dress according to his and the accepted code. The secretary sat silently as he spoke, but when he finished, she stood up and said quite pointedly, "Who needs this crap?" Then she walked out of his office, sat at her desk, and continued to work at a rate that surpassed that of any secretary he had ever had.

As he related the story, the businessman said there was nothing he could do about her impertinence, unless he wanted to hurt himself. He could fire her, of course, and really teach *her* a lesson, forcing her to take unemployment pay, a few weeks of vacation, and a job with a company that would not be as concerned with the way she dressed. But *he* would be the real loser. He would spend two or three weeks trying to find a suitable replacement, another three or four months trying to help her learn the job, and another six months blaming himself for letting his ego cost him a year's efficiency in his office. He kept his secretary.

The power that parents exerted over their families, teachers over their classes, and pastors over their congregations has gone the same way it has with employers. It has passed into the hands of people who refuse to be coerced, so much so that for years I have not met anyone in authority who didn't admit that he has less power than his predecessor did a decade earlier. Because of this growing spirit of self-reliance, any attempt to use force is usually more harmful than helpful, regardless of popular recommendations to win through intimidation or to apply more power.

To win consistently with people, you must learn and master new psychological methods for winning cooperation and commitment. I know of no other place to learn them except here, for I have developed them from different approaches to psychology over the past twenty years. You could spend several years in a graduate program in psychology of course. But even then you would find that each department usually stresses concepts which reflect its own behavioral philosophy while failing to adequately consider any which do not. In addition, a large part of what you would learn would be academic rather than practical, unless you went on to do work in a clinic or went into residency. By selecting wisely from all across the discipline, I have learned practical methods that will help you understand the importance of personality patterns, avoid conflicts regularly, and win the cooperation of many people in ways that they respond to in a positive manner.

Before you start using the methods in this book, you should realize that while many people have an increasing sense of independence, they *will* cooperate with you when you can help them feel good about doing so. Unfortunately, though they want to be self-reliant, many men and women continue to interact in the negative ways they learned in childhood and seldom reexamined. To help them feel good about cooperating with you, as a means of winning consistently with a growing number of people, *you* will have to make the revolutionary effort to use the new methods.

Actually, there are only two basic psychological attitudes you can hold as you relate to the people you want cooperation from. You can fight against learning new ways of coping, neglecting your ability to shape life the way you want it; or you can accept the methods that change has brought, adapt to people, and master new ways of reaching your goals.

If you remain defensive, the best you can do is to circle the wagons and fight a rearguard action against those who refuse to do as you demand of them, as long as your strength holds out, and as long as you avoid ulcers, heart failure, or emotional collapse. Then circumstances and more adaptable people will control your life. When you need to gain the personal commitment of a rebellious teenager, a surly worker, a reluctant lover, or an angry manager, you will have to accept what he is willing to offer you.

This route is already overcrowded with those who have no concept of what is happening or any idea of how to win interpersonal commitment, even though they think that they do. At least you will not be lonely since most of the people you know will still be going around in that circle for the next forty years or so. But you will not be living the rewarding, stimulating life which belongs to winners, the people who know what is happening and how to shape life the way they want it.

You will find as you apply the techniques revealed in this book that they become a normal part of your relationships with other people, a part that they do not understand but which they approve of and respond to readily. They will only recognize that you have become a more understanding, more rewarding person to live, work, and play with, a real winner in the true sense of the word, and they will be willing to give you a commitment you will find astonishing.

Throughout *Nice Guys Finish First* I have used words like "he," "him," and "his" when talking about men and women alike. It seems that the mother tongue has not kept pace with the massive social changes the women's movement has wrought. My use of these words was dictated by a desire to keep a simple sentence structure and no more.

PART ONE

Preparing
to Win

(Relating Warmly and Supportively)

CHAPTER ONE

Human
Motivation

You are not alone in wanting to gain the commitment of the men and women who can help you make life richer and fuller for yourself and for them as well. All through history, perceptive, competent people have discovered effective methods of managing interpersonal relationships. Some of them were very effective, since every history book is filled with the exploits of people who had the interpersonal power, charm, or intelligence to influence the men and women around them to do as they wanted.

Napoleon Bonaparte was such a person. Although it is true that he was not above using a "whiff of grapeshot" to bring an unruly mob to its senses, he more frequently used his knowledge of human behavior and personality exceedingly well in an era preceding academic psychology. He was intelligent enough to reward his soldiers consistently, promoting men from the ranks, until it was said that every private in his army carried a marshal's baton in his knapsack, hoping that the lightning of the Emperor's favor would strike. When Napoleon returned from exile on Elba, the very army which was sent to arrest him was won over to his cause once more and followed him to Paris: officers, generals, and all.

The moral of Napoleon's story is simple: that you should look after your own interests, since no one else will, but you must share the winnings or others will grow weary and will leave you to your fate, alone. You need to have people like you while you persuade them to do the things you want done. But to establish relationships that are mutually satisfying and therefore likely to continue, you must master ways of creating appropriate behavior when you need to.

Psychology can help you do this, though it isn't a single science, as many people think, but a loose confederation of researchers and practitioners who sometimes work together from the same theoretical framework and sometimes work in opposition to each other. In some colleges psychology is considered a biological science and in others it is a social science. With such different approaches to understanding human attitudes and behavior, each school of psychology has its own philosophy, traditions, and methods of coping with problems. Each school creates methods for dealing with certain types of difficulties. I have taken several methods from their traditional frameworks, and have woven them together into a single program in this book.

When the methods are combined they become what I call the Law of Psychological Reciprocity, perhaps the most useful concept ever developed for controlling the attitudes and behavior of people. By applying the Law of Reciprocity, you can develop a consistent reward system that enables people to find satisfaction by working with you rather than by trying to frustrate or ignore you.

The Law of Reciprocity

When men and women meet, they invariably go through a series of unspoken and often unconscious transactions that are a survival tactic from our primitive past. The transactions remain a part of our instinctive behavior, much as our social customs and traditions do. Even after we have learned that another person is safe, we still interpret each new encounter to verify our perception of the situation. The Law of Reciprocity can be summed up in these words:

THE WAY YOU WANT PEOPLE TO ACT TOWARD YOU
IS THE WAY YOU MUST FIRST TREAT THEM.

Men and women take their cues from each other because life is filled with spoken and unspoken tradeoffs that people require of each other. If we offer friendship, it is normally returned. If we are honest and sincere, people will be the same with us. If we are critical and harsh, they protect themselves in much the same manner. You only have to use the DeVille Sidewalk Test to see the Law of Reciprocity in operation.

The next time you walk down a crowded sidewalk, smile and nod at the people you meet. Almost everyone will return your greeting with a smile of his or her own, and many may wish you a good day as well. On the following block, frown and stare at the oncoming people, but be prepared to get out of their way. When I frown at people, I have had men and women stop and glare at me, swear aloud, clench their fists, and even step between parked cars to get away from me. They were hooking into my behavior according to the Law of Reciprocity.

There are men and women who have been so badly hurt in their relationships that they cannot relate to others in socially acceptable ways, regardless of how well they are treated. Included in this category are the mentally ill, confidence artists, muggers, and others who have failed to understand the cause-and-effect relationships that make life more rewarding. Their behavior is usually fixed in childhood, but some adults have been so badly hurt in business, marriage, or in selfish friendships that they are perpetually defensive.

Another group of people who do not almost automati-

cally react to the way they are being treated are the level-
headed, emotionally mature adults who understand the fears
and frustrations that produce the unpleasant acts committed
by others. We can all be hooked when we are tired, frustrated, or frightened, but emotionally mature, psychologically sophisticated men and women are often able to resist
a childlike response.

One grandfather I know understands this quite well.
John's daughter and son-in-law were going through a difficult time of separation and divorce. That was traumatic
enough in itself, but they started fighting over the custody
of their four-year-old daughter. The struggle became quite
bitter after a while and then seemed to lessen after Carl ap-
parently was reconciled to the fact that Shirley was going
to leave in spite of him. At that time, the young mother
was persuaded to send the child to her paternal grandmother's for a weekend. But when she returned on Monday
morning to get the child, the grandmother refused to surrender her without Carl's permission.

Shirley called John and they returned to the mother-in-
law's house. But rather than going to the front, Shirley
went around back of the home and tried to get the child
out without the older woman seeing her. She failed and the
two women became embroiled in a tugging match with
the child literally in the middle. They were screaming and
the child was crying when John followed, muscled his way
in, and took the child from both of them. He then led her
aside, where he sat on a garden bench to comfort her, as
he held her close. While the argument was still raging, Carl,
the child's father, drove up and jumped over the fence,
ready to do battle in his anger. He was furious with Shirley,
hurt at her leaving, and suspicious of the way she had tried
to get the child from his mother. He swore at her, threat-
ened her, and walked over to John to harshly demand his
daughter.

The grandfather stood, kissed the little girl gently, and handed her to her father. As the younger man took the child, John encircled both of them in his massive arms and spoke gently to Carl. He said:

> We cannot do this to our beautiful little girl. It seems to me that you and I'll have to keep our heads and settle this in a way that's best for her. Can I count on you? I don't think the women can do it right now. They're too upset.

John later said that the tension and anger went out of Carl like a balloon that was deflated. He kissed his daughter and nodded to his father-in-law. John and Shirley followed Carl to his apartment, and within an hour he had given her the child and his promise to return her without confrontations when she came on a visit. It happened because John understood that the way we treat people is the way they most often react toward us.

The different aspects of the Law of Reciprocity, for influencing the attitudes and behavior of people, can be combined into a single Basic Principle for you to use. It is this:

GOOD THINGS HAPPEN TO PEOPLE WHO COOPERATE.

Using the Basic Principle

This principle for winning almost universal cooperation and commitment is based on the three crucial factors in all human motivation. They form a simple but universal approach, since humans always follow them unless they are frightened, angry, or confused. According to Viktor Frankl, people always prefer:

> PLEASURE to Pain
> POWER or PRESTIGE to Devaluation
> PURPOSE to Futility

When you understand this progression to motivation and apply it as the Basic Principle, you can develop the most powerful motivation technique available. People all want to come through life being winners, so when you consistently use your skills to help them gain pleasure, prestige or power, and purpose, they will give you their cooperation. Men and women invariably want to feel good instead of bad, to feel important instead of unimportant, and to have a purposeful rather than a meaningless life. When you make it possible for them to experience these things through interpersonal cooperation, you will consistently have their loyalty and commitment.

The Basic Principle is effective because humans are self-centered. Each person wants to earn a reward for his investment of energy and time. With our unique human ability to substitute the symbolic for the tangible, these rewards may become psychological and spiritual rather than material. Adults are always too complex to be led to great achievements by offering them simple rewards. This is one of the mistakes made by some psychologists who try to control behavior at too low a level of motivation. Each person functions first at the material level, meeting those needs before moving upward to his psychological needs. He then experiences the spiritual aspects of his personality, and these must be satisfied in an entirely different fashion with a more sophisticated set of rewards.

You would think that everyone understands that people prefer a pat on the back to a kick lower down—winning in life to losing—but I am continually amazed at how few people appreciate the powerful interpersonal leverage a system built on this knowledge would give them. I continually see parents, teachers, ministers, and managers who don't say anything to the people they are trying to guide until something goes wrong. Then they attack them, thus assuring that the person who is hurt or humiliated will do his best in the future—not to improve, but to keep a future mistake from being discovered.

When I spoke to Paul, a store manager, about rewarding some of his employees with praise for working well, he frowned in obvious confusion, saying:

> I pay them to work like I want them to, not to have me hold their hands and wipe their noses. When they work well I leave them alone. When they don't I kick them in the butt. That motivates them!

Paul preferred a pat on the back to being devalued. But he couldn't see any connection between his feelings and his practice of ignoring his salespeople until they made a mistake. And following his assault *they* were not motivated, *he* was! He was the one with all his juices bubbling, his heart pounding, and his blood pushing through constricted arteries, setting the stage for the stroke or heart attack so many managers experience because they don't know how to gain the commitment people want to give to employers who know how to make them feel good about themselves and the relationship.

Each man and woman wants to be appreciated and shown that he is valuable to the group he works, plays, or studies with. I don't really know how to achieve this except to connect what people want and need to the pleasure, prestige, and purpose I can offer them. The methods taught in this book are doubly effective because they are so wholeheartedly approved of by the people you are using them with. These people want good things to happen to them even more than you want that for them.

Achieving pleasure, power or prestige, and purpose are the only motives you can rely on. The rewards that meet a person's needs are his *payoff* from life. They are the ultimate reasons he works, plays, loves, or does whatever he does. Not only do men and women accept any payoffs they chance upon, they actively seek them and carry out tasks that regularly give payoffs at the material, psychological, and spiritual levels. And like a person who dominates all his games, a person who wins by devaluing others, as Paul does, is soon playing solitaire.

Men and women expect the payoffs of life to balance out over the long run, even if specific days, weeks, or months fluctuate somewhat. As long as a person feels that he or she is winning his payoff regularly for his investment in a relationship, he continues to cooperate. If, however, he feels that he is giving more than he is receiving for his investment, he usually wants an adjustment.

When football superstar O. J. Simpson had a two-thousand-yard season, thus earning the owners an extra million dollars or so, he immediately asked for a more rewarding contract, despite the fact that he had already signed one for a lesser payoff. The team owner gave it to him with virtually no haggling, for he wanted O. J. to feel good about the relationship, especially since he would be a free agent in the near future.

When an adjustment is refused, however, the dissatisfied person is forced to do one of two things: he can accept the judgment that he or she really isn't worth the extra reward, or he can end the relationship, which he feels has become unbalanced. In a marriage this is called a divorce.

People who are strongly attracted to a particular level of motivation and payoff often fail to understand that others function on a different level. Not long ago more Harvard graduates were joining the Peace Corps than were going into business. They were looking for a higher level payoff than business corporations were offering them. So many young men and women have chosen careers in education, social work, and law that these fields have become crowded with professionals who are showing that the amount of money isn't so important after a certain level of comfort and consumption has been reached.

I have a friend who is very successful in a large computer manufacturing firm, being talented, articulate, and productive. About a year ago she expected a raise of about five thousand dollars because of the profits her group earned the previous year. Her manager, a corporate vice-president, was a very perceptive man, however. He offered her only twenty-five hundred dollars, a corner office, and her name on the stationery. My friend accepted, since the prestige was more important to her than anything she could buy with the money after taxes had riddled it.

In our affluent society her story is more common than many people recognize. For example, it is impossible to find a simple motive for two teen-age boys rushing into a burning house to rescue a man they don't know, but two of my son's friends did that recently, risking their lives in a selfless act of bravery. And when the United States Navy cruiser *Quincy* was sinking in World War II, four chaplains gave their life preservers to seamen when the ship was doomed. All four of the clergymen drowned, so the way one feels about himself is obviously a powerful behavior reinforcer.

Rewards that are offered to shape behavior must be matched to the level at which someone is functioning, since he will do what you ask of him for his own reasons and not yours. Few men and women are interested in breaking last year's sales record so you can have a trip to Hawaii. And they don't really care if you *ever* have a chalet in Vail. They are willing to help only when they see that doing so has some personal payoff, especially if that payoff is the way they feel about themselves.

Applying Payoffs Effectively

Fortunately for ambitious people who want to win in life, most men and women are wanting creatures, seldom satisfied for long with the payoffs they have already won, especially on the pleasure or power levels. For example, a person who takes a job and receives only money as his reward for going to work is not likely to give his commitment to the company. To gain consistent employee commitment, a manager has to move to a higher reward system by helping the worker feel good about being associated with the group, its goals, or whatever is important to the people. The same is true when a parent is trying to socialize a child or keep a teenager from doing things that would affect his growth negatively. Continual criticism will only make a child feel badly about himself, resent the parents, and give up on trying to become a winner. Correction is frequently needed, but it must always include acceptance of the child as well as suggestions of ways to improve unacceptable activities.

In the hundred years following Pavlov's animal research about conditioning, psychologists have developed some of the methods in this book. The control of a dog or a monkey is simple enough when shackles are used and the animal is deprived of food or water for several days preceding the experiment. When research is conducted with humans, the procedure is somewhat more complex, since imprisonment and starvation cannot be used except in institutions where the normal behavioral trade-offs have been suspended. This happens in prisons, mental hospitals, some military organizations, and some inner-city schools. There the members of the group are at the mercy of the staff, and experience has shown that compassion is a weak reed upon which to rely for support and justice. Nevertheless, men and women will respond to payoffs which are connected to their psychological and spiritual needs after their physical needs have been met.

I have two illustrations which show how the act of offering payoffs or reinforcement controls behavior. The first is about an animal I was training and the second about a professor I knew at one time.

One afternoon I set out to teach a young colt to come

when I summoned him with a loud whistle, since it was time for his training to start and I had no intention of chasing him all over the pasture when I wanted him. I led Dandy from the stall he shared with his mother, slipped a halter over his head, and took him outside the stable. I simply turned him loose and waited. The young animal went to the trough, drank his fill of water, and watched me for a few minutes. When I ignored him, he trotted out toward the pasture. As he did, I took a scoop of oats from the bin and waited for Dandy to return. In a few minutes he broke into a galloping circle and headed back toward the barn and his mother. As he moved toward me I was ready. I called his name loudly, whistled through my teeth, and rattled the scoop in the feed box. When he came to see what I had put in the box I gave him a handful of oats, praised him for being obedient, and scratched him thoroughly behind his ears. As he ate the oats he lost all interest on checking up on his mother, who continued to ignore us as she drowsed in the stall.

I went inside the stable, closed the door, and moved to a window where I could watch without being seen. Dandy stood by the door for a while, obviously hoping I would return with more oats, but I outwaited him. When he whinnied loudly a few times and I didn't respond, he galloped off once more, as I knew a frisky young animal would have to do. While he was making his circuit of the pasture, I went outside to call his name and whistle loudly once more, alternating the whistling and calling. With the memory of the oats and stroking fresh in his mind, the colt came at a gallop. I gave him oats, scratched and praised him once more, and returned to the stable. I had quite a struggle to get through the door without him, since I had become his payoff and Dandy had designs on me.

I had to wait longer for him to leave than previously, for he was beginning to get the picture, but he finally gave up and wandered off, no doubt completely puzzled by the irrationality of human nature. Dandy was across the pasture and moving in the opposite direction when I put my fingers in my mouth and whistled as loudly as I could. Instantly his head went up and he cut like a quarter horse, coming to me at a dead run, though my whistling had meant nothing to him a few minutes before. I gave him the last of the oats, praised him lavishly, and scratched behind his ears as he ate the grain.

In fifteen or twenty minutes I changed Dandy's behavior to suit myself and developed an affection that will last as long as we both live. Today the colt is a proud stallion with a bevy of mares in his harem, but I have only to stop my car beside the fence and whistle to have him abandon them and come at a gallop from as far as he can hear me, though I haven't fed him oats for seven years or more. I still pet and praise him, scratching behind his ears, though I have trouble reaching that high unless he lowers his head for me, and it is obvious that my acceptance has become more important to the ten-year-old stallion than a handful of oats.

In the second story, the setting was a psychology class in a liberal arts college. One semester, one of the more imaginative young women had a bright idea to end the professor's annoying habit of pacing to and fro on the stage as he lectured. The class had been studying the subject of behavior reinforcement and modification, so one day when the professor was a few minutes late for class, she got on the stage and outlined her plan.

The student instructed the group to lean slightly forward in their seats and to appear especially interested when the professor paced toward stage left, then to lean back and seem to lose interest when he paced toward stage right. The students were captivated, naturally, with any prospect of livening up the class with a game, so they agreed to cooperate. When the professor arrived a few minutes later the plan was put into effect without his knowing what was in store for him. It worked like a charm.

The following day the dean of the college called the psychology department chairman to ask why Dr. Davidson was lecturing his ten A.M. class from the left rear of the stage instead of from the podium as was customary. The puzzled chairman said that he had not the faintest idea, but he would check into the matter if the dean wished.

When questioned, Davidson looked a little embarrassed and bewildered and said that he couldn't explain what was happening, but suddenly, he stated, it seemed that his lecture was so much more effective from that location. A few more questions asked of the students gave the whole game away, and the story was told through the entire community.

Professor Davidson's need to do a good job with his students was great enough to make him accept their payoff, despite the fact that he was well aware of the reinforcement techniques used in psychology. The method is so rarely planned for or used in interpersonal relationships that he didn't realize it was being used on him. I certainly do not recommend that you use the approach in such a way as the students did, to humiliate someone. But the anecdote does show how powerful appropriate reinforcement can be in controlling decisions and behavior. When he found out what had happened, he took it in good grace, but other people might not. It certainly gave him some new insights, he admitted, into the feelings of his clients when he used behavior modification methods in therapy. That can lead to feelings of being manipulated, so you must always remain supportive as you create situations in which you can reward appropriate behavior.

When you use the process I have described to reward a person, you must keep three concepts in mind in order to be successful. The three are crucial whether you are trying to fix an acceptable behavior pattern or to end an unacceptable one. The first concept is, according to B. F. Skinner:

> THE PAYOFF MUST BE GIVEN AS SOON AS POSSIBLE
> AFTER THE APPROPRIATE BEHAVIOR IS PRODUCED.

It would have been useless to appear interested in the lecture until Davidson was moving in the right direction or to wait until he had finished speaking for the hour. It had to be connected in such a way that he understood the relationship even if he did not know why it was happening. If too much time is allowed to pass, and the reason for the reward is forgotten or has lost its urgency, much of the payoff's power to change behavior is lost. Of course, people can postpone their rewards much longer than animals can, as happens with medical students or authors, who often have to work for years without earning any income from their work. It is obvious, however, that students and writers are receiving some kind of payoff from their efforts, or they would drop out of school or put the typewriter away, like many people do.

The second concept to remember is:

> THE MORE A PERSON VALUES A PAYOFF,
> THE MORE IT WILL CONTROL HIS BEHAVIOR.

This is another one of those simple but profound statements that many people overlook because of their preoccupation with money as the major reward of life, especially in business or industry. I will work harder for a thousand dollars than I will for a hundred, but I do have some serious reservations because I have other values that are crucial to my life. I would not sell heroin to anyone, regardless of the profit I could make. Neither would I go to Saudi Arabia for an oil company, but for a different reason. I have a son who is finishing high school in the coming year and I want to be with him as he takes part in school activities, plays football, and becomes a delightful young man. The amount of money an Arabian company would pay me would be unimportant compared to that.

This doesn't change the fact that a payoff offered at the proper time will have a strong effect on our choices, according to the values the recipient places on it. You have only to watch the enthusiasm and creativity with which the contestants compete on television game shows to see this. The money they win is important, of course, but a perceptive person can see more than that desire at work. The contestants are also competing for status and self-esteem, as evidently the home viewers do also, since they are not winning any money except vicariously.

With a strong enough payoff at the appropriate level, virtually any personal attitude can be shaped, though you will have to remain supportive rather than become manipulative, and you must decide which level is most appropriate at the time.

The third concept to remember is:

REINFORCERS MUST BE GRANTED ONLY WHEN THE DESIRED BEHAVIOR IS OFFERED, AND WITHHELD AT ALL OTHER TIMES.

This is the practical connection of the payoff to the Basic Principle, that good things happen to people who work well together and cooperate. It is also implicit that bad things do not happen to people who will commit themselves to you. I'm not implying that you have the power to remove all the hurt and evil from the world, but that you will live by this principle in your relationships to the best of your ability. You are promising to cooperate with and reward people who help you, to refuse payoffs to those who do not, and to avoid hurting or humiliating employees, students, children, or relatives who try to help, simply because you are frustrated or unhappy with someone else.

Most men and women try to behave this way with those who are important to them. But few of the millions who try ever succeed in building these concepts into a personal system that makes them consistent winners. You must make your rewards contingent upon good things happening to both sides in the relationship. Surely you have already learned how important this is!

I long ago decided that it is better to pay my son for raking leaves or shoveling snow *after* the task is complete than to advance the money and then try to get the job done. There is less chance of an unhappy outcome, better work is done at a faster rate, and there is less argument about when it should be done if I do my good thing—paying up— after he has done his good thing—the work. There is less wear and tear on my nervous system than there would be if I tried to get him to pay for a dead horse, so to speak. My son is not at all unusual, for it is within the parameters of human nature to expect a reward for our activities, even when we love each other as my son and I do. It is not selfishness but simply a survival trait that the race still holds.

If we selfishly use the Basic Principle without concern for the feelings and needs of other people, we are effectively defeating our own purposes, winning the battles of the moment while losing the campaign for understanding and interpersonal commitment. Once a person feels he is being manipulated, whether you intended keeping all the rewards or not, he will go away in disgust, leaving you the loser that most manipulators eventually become. You need to establish an ongoing mutually beneficial relationship with the people you want to lead, building trust and support that extends to both of you. Of course, I find that you can do this more rapidly than normally happens by using the methods I have developed.

When you gain commitment by dealing from a strong, supportive value system and positive expectations, you will find it easier to be consistent with your rewards. They have become an extension of what you are at the core of your being rather than merely techniques that you have learned. It is virtually impossible for anyone to fool people about their motives for very long. A basic law of psychology is that men and women interpret nonverbal communication more readily than words that are spoken. This happens because each of us learned to interpret moods and acts from our parents before we learned to speak. And when a conflict or discrepancy exists between what we hear being said and what we feel nonverbally, the older, most basic form usually wins out. In short, as the old saw states, what you are speaks so loudly that people cannot hear what you say.

The Basic Principle in Operation

There are four steps to be followed in using the Basic Principle to win appropriate performance and commitment. They are:

1. *Identify* which behavior will be reinforced and what will please you.
2. *Determine* how often an undesired act is happening so you can tell whether you are using rewards successfully.
3. *Connect* the payoff to the desired behavior.
4. *Check* from time to time to observe how well the method is working.

Here are some samples of how effective payoffs can become when they are connected to appropriate acts and attitudes.

Identify: Dianne was a hardworking but frequently tardy secretary who worked for Roger in a hardware firm. Her habit of coming in late inconvenienced as well as annoyed him, because he liked to start his day by dictating the letters he had outlined in his head the previous afternoon.
Determine: Roger checked the times she had been tardy

on his calendar and found that she averaged twice weekly for three weeks.

Connect: Roger discussed the problem with Dianne and made her annual pay raise contingent upon her reducing her tardiness to no more than once a month. She didn't like the idea and he would have preferred perfection, but he accepted a realistic and more human solution. He remained firm about the once-a-month limit, however, despite her protests.

Check: Dianne's tardiness remained at the twice weekly average and slipped to three on the third week, so Roger spoke to her about it once more. He reminded her that her raise was still contingent upon her improved performance. *Good things don't happen to people who don't cooperate* was the message he gave her. After that her tardiness ended with just one relapse two months later. He granted the raise and that was the end of the matter. It was crucial that Roger be consistent and true to his word, or the process would have failed.

Identify: Jane and Josie, two teen-age sisters, were letting their room become cluttered with shoes, books, and junk, to the displeasure of their mother. Her repeated complaints and threats resulted in no improvement, and after working all day in the city the mother had no inclination to do the work herself.

Determine: The mother counted an average of ten or twelve items per day on the floor or bed over a two-week period.

Connect: The mother brought an old chest down from the attic, painted it to match the decor of the room, and had a key made to fit the lock. After a family conference about the problem, each daughter was given the responsibility of taking care of her own things. Anything the mother found scattered around would go into the box where it would be locked away until one hour following breakfast on Saturday morning. The Saturday Box would be opened for half an hour and any impounded item could be recovered at that time.

Check: After two weeks of using the Saturday Box with firmness despite threats to commit suicide, and run off to Alaska, the littering decreased to an average of three items per week. This method is very effective for everyone from kindergartners to husbands. Having to wait until the Saturday opening for the football forecasts will certainly make most husbands quite conscious of where they put the paper after dinner.

Identify: Donald Hendon was the principal of a large city school in New England. He was a few years from retirement and the three assistant principals were competing for his job. The recurring conflicts among the two men and one woman had become increasingly unpleasant, yet he wanted to end it without decreasing the ambition or the drive of his assistants.

Determine: It seemed to Dr. Hendon that some conflict was breaking out almost every time they met, though he never counted the times. He did know that it was happening all too often for him to accept.

Connect: After one severe confrontation he called the assistant principal who had been less disruptive and contentious to his office, and said, "Cal, I liked the way you refused to be baited by Herb and Janet today. It showed real maturity on your part so keep up the good work." At the next meeting Cal was less argumentative than before and even a little smug about it. And because so much human behavior hinges around the Law of Reciprocity, the second or third time Janet launched an attack that Cal coolly ignored, she was forced to examine what was happening. This pause in the conflict gave Donald a chance to tell her the same thing. "Janet, you're handling yourself better now with Cal and Herb. There's less time wasted in our meetings and I like your new way better." Herb was slower to catch on that things were changing but in time he paused enough for the principal to get to him with a psychological payoff.

Check: In two weeks the conflicts disappeared and the three assistants learned the extent of the competition the principal could tolerate without his humiliating them or blunting their ambition to succeed him.

CHAPTER TWO

Creatures
of Habit

Not only do men and women live according to the Law of Psychological Reciprocity, taking their cues from the people they meet and the situations they enter, they also follow the Law of Psychological Economy in their lives. This second law evolved in order to save time and energy in routine activities and relationships. Once you have learned to drive a car, swim, ride a bicycle, or to interpret the moods and actions of other people, you follow the Law of Economy to simplify your life and to reduce the number of conscious decisions you have to make.

In the vast majority of your decisions, this is not only good, it is necessary if you are not to be overwhelmed with trivia. Problems arise when you automatically behave in the same way you always have even though it is no longer effective for you to do so. But in any case, you live within the patterns you find comfortable, though in this age of change, when instincts and traditions no longer serve you well, your habits get you into trouble. You go on doing what you have always done, largely to reduce tension, and then discover to your dismay that people are no longer will-

ing to let you share in the winnings. You fail to realize that
you have become like the best buggy-whip maker in town:
skilled, respected, and out of work. However, there are
valid reasons why people still cling to the concepts and
methods they learned in the past, why they behave defen-
sively rather than accepting others.

Childhood Conditioning

Men and women have always known that people around
them act with consistency as they relate to others, even
when they live with the illusion that they are somehow different, that they are personally very flexible and able to
modify their own style of coping. At a family reunion,
everyone knows that practical joker Uncle John will still
be pulling pranks as he has done for fifty years, Aunt Bess
will still be criticizing the younger generation, and Grandfather Tom will be out playing ball with the boys and girls
instead of gossiping around the punchbowl with people his
own age.

As long ago as the Golden Age of Greece, Aristotle
developed his concept of human temperaments as a means
of interpreting and predicting human behavior. In the last
two thousand years other philosophers and theologians have
done the same thing, though in the last century the interest
has shifted to psychologists and psychiatrists, whose work
is to assess the behavior of men and women. A number of
researchers such as Merrill have taken the knowledge to a
new level, showing with research that people do indeed
live within clearly defined patterns, going far beyond the
simple concepts of Aristotle, Jung, and Freud.

Contemporary researchers have discovered that each person has a predictable personality pattern which starts to
form early in life, perhaps as early as the fourth or fifth
month, and is completely jelled by the third or fourth year

of life. At the present time no one can say what percentage of a person's behavioral pattern is inherited through his genes and what proportion is learned from the events and relationships of his formative years. But the patterns with which each person goes through life are set before he starts school in all but the most unusual cases. And it is really unimportant what percentage came from which source, for a person is forced to deal interpersonally with other people as he is in adulthood, not as he might have been if his parents had acted differently.

Each pattern is so predictable that a basic axiom of psychotherapy is that a counselor or therapist must look for major shifts in a person's pattern, since this is frequently a sign of pressure and possibly of approaching emotional disorder. While an emotionally stable person is usually more flexible than a disturbed one, extreme flexibility doesn't improve interpersonal relationships, since other people don't expect it. They are well aware that people behave in patterns, and if someone suddenly changes his pattern drastically, he will come across as a shifty or slippery character.

Anyone who has ever reared children realizes that they are all born unhousebroken little apes, as Robert Benchley wrote so wittily, who require fifteen or twenty years of intensive socialization to be converted into people! And even then some parents are not successful. This constant conditioning isn't necessarily pleasant to the child, since he wants what he wants when he wants it. Socialization can be done with the use of reinforcement from a loving heart as described in Chapter One, or it can be accomplished with a slap to the mouth when the child makes a mistake. The trouble with the latter approach is that the child doesn't perceive whether the parent is simply angry or severely frustrated, and therefore doesn't learn what the limits of acceptable behavior are. He will have no sense of how to cope with people in a winning manner. But he does learn things that the parents don't intend: to use the Law of the Jungle in his relationships, to use stealth and cunning as he attacks weaker people in turn.

Just a few days ago I was talking to a father who insisted that the only way his children could learn to get along in life was to obey him immediately, without question, when he spoke. I tried to show him how disastrous this would be for a child who didn't learn to evaluate the obligations people would place on him as he grew to adulthood, how being conditioned to obey without question would make him vulnerable to every swindler, confidence artist, and manipulator he met. Each person has to learn to say "no" to the demands made upon him far more often than he agrees to what other people want him to do. If he gives other people a payoff every time they ask, he is reinforcing their demands upon him until ultimately he is overwhelmed with obligations.

In the socialization of a child, the wise parent will strike a balance as he teaches the youngster to survive in a world that is crowded and that will not tolerate blatant selfishness from young adults. Each society punishes people who act at twenty or twenty-five as they did at two or three. Criminals and psychopaths who cannot postpone gratification are put into prisons or mental hospitals largely because they have not matured emotionally.

But while socialization is necessary for survival as an adult, the childhood conditioning never follows a logical, psychologically consistent pattern in any family. Both parents grew up differently, learning their styles of relating within families to which their own parents brought different attitudes and expectations of what was effective, valuable, and decent. Long before the young adults can get their own differences sorted out, they have their children, forcing the next generation to struggle along, learning from each other, making compromises, maintaining some traditions they assume are right and proper for all people. Parents give orders to the children, use punishment, and offer rewards until each family finally jells in its particular fashion, a mix which may be effective in teaching children to deal successfully with other people and which may not, forcing the children to cope with life with inadequate tools.

This is one reason why people experience so many interpersonal failures today, a problem which rarely existed in simpler, less mobile societies. For example, at one time Native American children grew up in the same society, holding the same values and expectations, having the assurance that life was going to remain the same for their children for as long as the grass would grow and the buffalo would roam. It was such a stable way of life that the Native Americans didn't even know what mental illness was.

In present-day society, divorces and remarriages expose children to different family mixes. This, combined with increasing mobility, has made the socialization of children even more of a patchwork affair of myths, lies, half-truths, and half-lies. As the child grows up in this shifting world, frequently confused by irreconcilable parental admonishments and expectations, he does his best to adapt and to make sense out of life. He tries to learn ways of coping with events and relationships that meet his self-centered needs, but that don't get him into too much trouble with others who are just as self-centered as he is. The child usually learns to use a personality pattern that is acceptable to himself and the people around him without causing too much tension or conflict. This pattern, of which he is unaware, enables him to live comfortably—to remain in his emotional comfort zone—as he interacts with others. His comfort zone is the personal span of attitudes and acts from which he gets the most done with the least expenditure of psychic energy.

Some children learn to be watchful of others, trying to comprehend as much as they can before they act to solve their problems. Other children learn to be little showmen, entertaining others with a smile and a song, which is intended to put important people in a better mood. Some try to cope by telling other people what to do, becoming Mommy's or Daddy's little second-in-command, identifying with the controlling powers of the world. Still others learn to be quietly accepting, to please the people around them by being supportive and helpful in the relationships they share.

Each child is only doing what works best for winning his material or psychological payoff in the particular mix of people, events, and traits he has to cope with during his childhood conditioning period. It is the only way he can survive and grow up undisturbed, and that is all there is to it. No one way of dealing with other people is better than any other, though people normally assume that their own way is the best. It was evidently best in childhood, but that's no longer true in adult life, for you are dealing with a much broader mix of people. And the payoffs of life are considerably different!

While the child was learning to cope and being rewarded for using an acceptable mode of behavior, it became his automatic way of dealing with others. If he was fortunate enough to learn that his is only one way of several, he can be accepting of people who are different. If, however, he learned that his was the only "right way," because of pressures that made him rigid through excessive punishment or overcontrol, he may have reached adulthood as a social cripple. He will not be able to deal effectively with the three quarters of the human race who are different from himself, all those men and women who have learned to use different personality patterns, the people who are determined to remain in their own comfort zones instead of adapting to meet his needs, thus remaining beyond his power to influence them.

Personality Patterns

Each person unconsciously attempts to remain in his personal comfort zone as much as possible as he works, plays, worships, or loves with other people. To remain comfortable he takes his cues from the people around him as well as from his inner conditions at the time, following both the Law of Reciprocity and the Law of Economy. If he guesses correctly, he can adjust somewhat, but still remain in his comfort zone. To make it easier to interpret the actions of other people, each adult has a set of categories in which he places others as a means of helping him predict behavior economically. Men and women tend to stereotype, classifying some people as blabbermouths, tyrants, high rollers, cheapskates, and so on, following the Law of Economy.

This stereotyping seems instinctive, since all people do it regularly in new relationships. In fact, no one in any of my seminars has ever denied having his own private method, which he has used from the time he first realized that people are different from each other in crucial ways. But since your private categories are largely based on childhood learning and serve a defensive rather than an accepting purpose, this personal system usually leaves you too self-centered, too disorganized, and too immature to be of consistent help.

To compound your problems in predicting and controlling the acts of other people, you often judge their acts when they are putting pressure on you, forcing you out of your comfort zone and putting you in a poor position to make a decision about another person. A young man in one of my seminars told of how he had done this with his wife's sister.

Tom first met Dorothy when he had gone home with his fiancée for the first time. He said:

I discovered what you are talking about a few years ago, though I didn't understand the reason for it until I attended this seminar. We met my wife's folks and I found they were fine people. I did have a personality conflict with her sister, Dorothy, however. She's a nurse, and we got off on the wrong foot at the very beginning. My sense of comfort includes being friendly, telling jokes, and dominating the conversation with my repertory of stories—a real Entertainer, to use your term. Unfortunately, her pattern was directly opposite to mine, for she was quiet and introspective. And the harder I worked to make her accept me with my jokes and stories, the more she considered me a blabbermouth.

I could not become comfortable with her, and I kept her off balance as well. I felt she was a cold fish with no sensitivity to my position. And obviously she felt I was a chowderhead with a joke book for a brain. We related so badly that she even tried to stop Susan from marrying me, so you can imagine how we felt about each other after that. It was all downhill for several years.

Then Susan had a miscarriage and Dorothy and I were thrown together when complications set in and we needed her nursing skills. And I finally discovered the real person hidden behind our conflict in personality patterns. That "cold fish" was a loving sister who cared more for her kid sister than words could ever tell. She kept us from falling apart in that crisis. And my growing respect for her let her abandon her defenses to see me in a different light, still too talkative to suit her personally, but a good husband who loves her sister dearly. We've become good friends now, though I try to tone down my exuberance when she's around.

For the past twenty years Merrill and Wilson have invested a great amount of effort studying the human need to classify people, conducting more than 125,000 evaluations of men and women from all jobs and walks of life. They used a questionnaire which several acquaintances of each subject filled out, checking off words that described his personal pattern of interpersonal interaction for remaining in his comfort zone.

As they analyzed the half-million questionnaires, the researchers first discovered that some people prefer competing in their relationships, while others prefer cooperating. They also found that some people are strongly competitive while others are only mildly so. When they plotted the cooperative traits, they found a similar distribution. On a simple scale that ranges from very cooperative to highly competitive, the results look like this, with about 25 percent of all men and women fitting in each block.

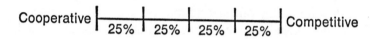

The researchers found that people with strong competitive traits have the ability to express their beliefs, desires, and choices openly and forcefully. The closer to the center of the scale their peers placed them, the less forceful are their own ideas and choices. The people at the other end of the scale, the cooperative end, are most able to get along with other men and women.

Cooperative people appear thoughtful, well organized, and willing to negotiate solutions to problems and conflicts. Notice that all these traits are positive. This means that there is no good or bad place on the scale, despite what you think when you are being forced from your comfort zone by someone who has the power or wit to do so. Then you face the temptation to make your judgment about him, and it is rarely a positive one, especially if the other person has been forced out of his zone and is acting abnormally in response to you, as he tries to get back to his normal manner of dealing interpersonally.

A competitive person is usually willing to tell others what he wants them to do, much as President Harry Truman or Senator Hubert Humphrey did. You may not agree with a competitive person, but you usually know what he is thinking about. This forceful method of communicating is his way of getting rid of interpersonal tension before he is driven from his comfortable way of interacting.

Sometimes, a competitive person will try to assert himself when he shouldn't, before he has all the facts or before he has won the rapport of people he is trying to lead or to convince to do as he wants. Thus he causes problems for himself and for others as well.

A cooperative person is usually easygoing in appearance, avoids dominating others emotionally, and frequently keeps his own counsel as a means of remaining comfortable. Such a person frequently goes out of his way to avoid seeming to control the emotions and behaviors of others, and may not talk to people unless he has something to communicate.

As you make judgments of the people you meet, there are a number of signs you can look for as you try to determine whether they are cooperative or competitive. If a person seems comfortable with power when dealing with people, remaining at a storm center much of the time, arguing his points with a dominant voice, he can be classified as a competitive person. If a person is subtle in the use of personal power, takes few risks, and avoids confrontations when possible, he is likely to be cooperative in nature.

The position each person occupies on the scale, from highly competitive to deeply cooperative, depends on the traits he inherited and on the learning that occurred in childhood. It has nothing to do with honesty, mental health, leadership ability, or intelligence, though our society has a number of cultural myths that link personality patterns to effectiveness. Many a cooperative young woman has made the mistake of assuming that a competitive man was more masculine and more virile as a lover, only to discover after a few months of marriage that she had believed a myth that had no relationship to reality.

The second set of traits discovered by the researchers as they interpreted their enormous amount of data was the degree to which personal reaction informed the events and relationships each person faces throughout life. These traits are self-control and self-expression.

The more a person expresses himself, the easier it is to understand his feelings, whether they are love, hate, anger, or fear. A highly expressive man or woman is one who indulges his emotions, who is willing to share them openly and freely with the people around him. He is willing to be the star in a relationship, and will even demand to be highly visible, to be applauded and appreciated. In addition, he or she is willing to accept the feelings of other people as important to the relationship. Therefore he is likely to be rather informal and feels free to express his feelings quickly. This quick familiarity may offend those who are more self-controlled, as it did one woman who wrote Dear Abby protesting the easy familiarity of so many people who use her given name without her permission.

The self-controlled person is not comfortable revealing his deeper feelings, therefore he does not seem as deeply concerned about emotions, either his own or those of others. He may give the impression that he is unaware of how other people feel about him, being more interested in what people think and do rather than in what they feel.

A self-controlled person may seem cold and too formal because he keeps people at an emotional distance, unless they have become close friends or at least acquaintances he has known for a long time. He may give the impression of being cold and calculating when a friend or relative needs consolation or support, unless people who are more self-expressive understand that he is only remaining in his comfort zone. His persisting pattern of not responding to social amenities can hurt the feelings of people who are more self-expressive than he.

Comedians Johnny Carson and Carol Burnett are good examples of self-expressive people. They are quite willing to share their feelings with millions of people through the medium of television. Actors Gary Cooper and John Wayne are examples of self-controlled people. When the traits are plotted from the surveys, the distribution of characteristics looks like this.

As on the first scale, there is no best place to be. Each person's position has nothing to do with emotional maturity, motivation, ability, or commitment. It has nothing to do with actual feelings, either, but rather with the outward expression of a person's emotions. Once again, however, American mythology dictates that children learn that grim, silent men are more effective than talkative ones, though weaker women and children can be permitted more self-expression. This is total nonsense.

One of the major discoveries of the psychologists conducting the research is the remarkable consistency with which people filling out the questionnaires place the person being evaluated. When people from different aspects of life, work, school, church, or the Thursday night poker club complete the questionnaire without knowing each other, they virtually always place the subject in about the same location. Your habits are too strong and your comfort zones are too important for you to shift around like a chameleon to meet the expectations of people around you. You are able to shift for a short while, at an increase in tension, but as soon as you stop thinking about being different, you unconsciously drop back into your own interpersonal comfort zone. You do, however, think that you can shift your pattern much more than you actually can.

Think about one of your friends and the way he acts most of the time. Does he prefer competing or cooperating at work and at play? If he prefers competing hard on the tennis court, does he stop competing when working on the job? Or do you see the consistency revealed by psychological research as well as by observation, a consistency in him that you have come to rely on?

When the two scales are combined, they form a figure that looks like this:

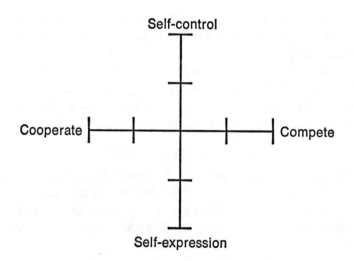

In actual practice, the scales form a chart on which the terms are changed to be somewhat more appropriate. It looks like this:

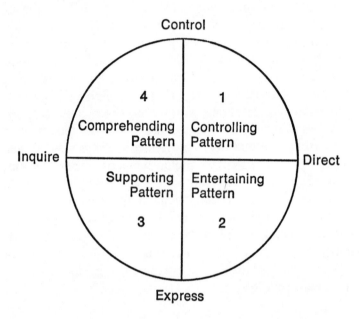

Starting at sector 1 and moving around in a clockwise direction, you can now see the four basic personality patterns the researchers have identified among the 125,000 profiles plotted from research instead of from cultural or personal assumptions. Understanding the needs and the predictable patterns of people who fall in each sector will be of great value in persuading people to do as you want.

The Controlling Pattern

In sector 1 you can recognize the personality pattern of a man or a woman who combines *directing* others with *control* of his emotions. Being a competitive and self-controlled person, he is assertive and somewhat extroverted.

This is the *Controlling* pattern and it is used by the men and women who are the Command specialists of society. Henry Ford II and Billy Graham are examples of the Controlling pattern.

The Entertaining Pattern

The traits found in sector 2 identify people who are willing to *direct* people the way Controllers do, but who are far more *expressive* in their activities and in their relationships. They have few inhibitions about making their feelings known. Rather than seeing any value in controlling their feelings, they are more comfortable when sharing their emotions as they tell others about their likes and dislikes. They are the Emotive specialists of life, who relate quickly to strangers and are willing to dominate scenes, but who are not so willing to share the spotlight. Joan Rivers and Johnny Carson use the *Entertaining* pattern as they cope and relate.

The Supporting Pattern

The characteristics found in sector 3 include *inquiring* and *expressing* to form a distinctly different pattern of personality. Much like Entertainers, men and women in this sector are concerned about emotions, but are not so competitive in expressing them. They are willing to inquire about the feelings of other people rather than to discuss what they are feeling themselves. Not being as assertive, they focus on the aspects of life that cause other people to feel good or bad about themselves. They are the Concern specialists of life, who reach their goals by dealing warmly with people they would like to make into friends. They go out of their way to avoid conflicts, since cooperation rather than competition keeps them from becoming uncomfortable. Ed McMahon of the Tonight Show and Dinah Shore are *Supporters*.

The Comprehending Pattern

The final personality pattern combines the traits of *control* and *inquiry* by people who prefer cooperating to competing, but who are not willing or able to express their feelings freely. In the expression of emotions they are more like Controllers, at the top of the chart. They are not as assertive, however, being more interested in discovering what is happening rather than in directing others what to do. People with the *Comprehending* pattern are the Information specialists of life, since only a great deal of data will keep them comfortable. News commentator Eric Sevareid and Senator George McGovern exemplify Comprehenders.

There is no best place to be, since each person is only doing what he learned was best for him in childhood. And since no one deliberately wants to be uncomfortable, each person continues to live with the pattern he found the most effective for him. But while each person's pattern is automatic and normal, it can cause severe interpersonal strain for people who have no idea of what is taking place.

Trouble becomes most frequent when two people, in total ignorance of personality patterns, meet each other with a grim determination to remain in their own comfort zones come hell, high water, or the total collapse of the relationship. This happens when parents become dissatisfied with what the family mix has forced a particular child to become, blaming the child for not being what they want, when the pressures have come from them all along. It also happens when managers are determined to make employees adopt their own patterns or when teachers do the same with students, rewarding only those who allow them to remain in their comfort zone and penalizing those who do not.

On occasion you will meet a person who is so rigid that

he cannot adapt with any success. He or she would be in the outer margin of the chart, reminding one of Don Knotts, the comedian, who is hyperactive, or of Vince Lombardi, former coach of the Green Bay Packers football team, who was so directive and self-controlled that his players actually feared him.

When Robert Skoronski was offensive-line captain of the Packers in their championship era under Lombardi, he had an experience with the Controller coach which makes my point. He told of taking his family to an ice-cream parlor one night. He bought each child, his wife, and himself a cone, but as they were walking back to their car, Lombardi approached them. Skoronski greeted the man he had successfully played for over a ten-year period and received only an expressionless grunt in return. Then the man realized that he, a thirty-five-year-old professional, with half-grown kids, and a prosperous business of which he was the president, was hiding the ice-cream cone behind his back like a kid caught at the cookie jar.

If anyone was going to adjust to make the relationship prosper, it was *not* going to be Lombardi. He was too close to the outer edge for that. Obviously such a person is difficult to relate to, for he is strongly convinced that his way is the only "decent" way for anyone to behave.

Personality-Pattern Weaknesses

A Controller can become so impatient with more introspective people that he starts manipulating them or giving autocratic commands, which causes resentment and resistance in this age when commitment cannot be commanded. His shell of unresponsiveness may keep other people at such a distance that they fail to tell him what he needs to know to make his interpersonal activities prosper. If he is not careful he can become a jungle fighter who succeeds at first and then is taken from ambush because no one will tell him where the booby traps are hidden.

When Entertainers get into trouble it is frequently because they try to do too many things without organizing or ranking them according to their importance. Such a person can waste so much time discussing his dreams that he is not aware that the time for making them come true is long past. At times an Entertainer's flippant opinions on virtually every subject will alienate the men and women who understand their own fields well enough to recognize his shallow grasp of facts. He is like the Controller in that his willingness to take risks without enough knowledge can harm his family, class, church, or business.

Supporters often spend too much time relating, sharing opinions, and soothing feelings rather than probing for facts when they are important for decision making. Because a Supporter often makes his choices based on interpersonal trust, he can become vulnerable to a smooth-talking confidence man. The disciplining of children or friends on the job may be avoided for too long as he yields to his emotions rather than insisting on appropriate performance. A Supporter may miss some outstanding opportunities because he has spent too much time relating and not enough doing his homework, avoiding risks because of his need to feel safe and loved rather than respected and obeyed.

Comprehenders may create conflicts by avoiding personal relationships with people who need and expect them, procrastinating while analyzing recommendations and solutions to death, or seeming to be indecisive, as Senator McGovern looked in his presidential bid. If he or she is not careful, a Comprehender may be perceived as a nervous old maid who demands certainty in a world that doesn't offer it very often. A person with this pattern will often do very well as he strives to minimize errors and risks.

Keep in mind that all of the personality patterns can be equally effective and useful as long as the person understands and accepts the traits of the people he must relate to—acknowledging them to be equally as valid as his own. Each pattern has certain weaknesses and strengths that must be accounted for in persuading other people to help you reach your goals.

CHAPTER THREE

Identifying
Personality Patterns

When a person first learns about personality patterns, he usually has no idea of how he is perceived by others, for his use of traits is largely unconscious. I learned that I had a totally incorrect picture of my personality pattern. It wasn't until I interpreted my own profile that I had a clear understanding of what it is. Because I had taught for many years with good evaluations, I assumed that I was a talkative Entertainer. After all, I know many jokes and anecdotes, which I weave into my programs with considerable success. Besides that, when I was growing up, my father had always told me that I talked too much.

When my peers from different areas of my life filled in the questionnaires from which my profile was plotted, they ignored my stage personality, focusing, as they were supposed to, on my interpersonal style of dealing with other people on a one-to-one basis. They all agreed, though they didn't know each other, that I was a Supporter with some Controlling tendencies, that I was extremely concerned about feelings and rather cooperative, though I do need to have tasks finished on schedule. My Entertaining style

60

is only an act that I perform when I am teaching or lecturing.

Most people are as ignorant about themselves as I was, so they remain in the dark, unable to successfully shift their patterns for the simple reason that they don't know what the starting point is. In addition to that lack of knowledge, most people have been misled by social myths about the effectiveness of patterns, so they expect that one or another is better. This is a result of unscientific stereotyping: people expect certain traits from Jewish mothers, scientists, politicians, actors, and doctors, characteristics that have nothing to do with reality. Because they expect the myths or else simply ignore any information that contradicts their expectations, they frequently cause problems for themselves. They expect people to fit their convenient categories.

A year or so ago I was conducting a seminar to teach managers how to apply personality-pattern knowledge for a group of twenty-four corporate vice-presidents. After we had been in session for several hours, what I was saying penetrated the mind of a Controlling style vice-president of a prominent meat-packing firm in Chicago. He unintentionally revealed how damaging the myths of our society can be when we act as if they are true. John interrupted me to ask a question in his dominant, self-controlled voice, saying:

> Do you mean to say that you believe a man can be successful in business without being competitive and emotionally self-controlled?

I told him that I meant just that, but I spoke softly in my unchallenging Supporter style.

> A person's success or failure in business, education, or child-rearing has virtually nothing to do with his pattern, providing he learns to accept the patterns other people use and to adapt when he needs to.

John immediately expressed his disagreement in no uncertain terms. He snapped:

> That's nonsense. No one can succeed in business unless he competes like hell and conceals his feelings from others.

The group of men and women digested his statement silently, but they were watching closely to see how I would handle the Controller's challenge. Fortunately, before starting the course, I had familiarized myself with all the profiles as well as with their careers. I countered with a question of my own: "Would you mind repeating that to Roger over there?" I pointed to a large, blond Scandinavian man who had sat silently through the preceding discussions, though he seemed interested and accepting of the rest of the class. He simply had not volunteered any information or asked any questions.

John countered with a question in turn. "Why?"

Instead of answering, I spoke directly to the large man: "What's your personality pattern, Roger?"

He smiled—shyly, I thought—and made a conciliatory gesture toward John, for he was going to disagree with him and could see where I was leading the conversation. "I'm a Supporter."

I persisted, however. "What's your job?"

"I'm senior vice-president of North Star Mining, but I'll become chief operations officer next June."

I had to turn the knife to make my point, so I pressed on. "How many people are you responsible for?"

"About seventy-five hundred miners and support people."

I continued to probe. "How on earth does a quiet, soft-spoken Supporter get any work out of a hard-rock crew like that, out on the edge of civilization? Mining operations are tough business."

Roger smiled proudly, like a schoolboy reciting a lesson. "I don't have any trouble. We've got a good bunch of fellows on our team. We work hard, but we cooperate. If any of my managers gets into trouble, he comes to me and we work things out. None of the boys ever let me down. We trust each other, and it works well for North Star."

I turned back to John and asked how many employees he had in his profit center. He looked at Roger and then back to me with an obvious sense of confusion as he slowly admitted to having less than a tenth as many as Roger had. Then he brightened and said that while Roger's pattern might be effective on the Iron Range of Minnesota, it would never work in Chicago.

What he was saying was that Roger's pattern would never be accepted in his meat-packing company. He was probably right about that—John is an intelligent, perceptive man—but not for the reasons he assumed. Roger's pattern wouldn't work in John's company because company executives had consciously or unconsciously decided that only Controllers are effective leaders. They had organized a self-fulfilling prophecy that kept anyone with another pattern from proving himself. Unfortunately, many schools, churches, families, and businesses do the same thing.

One of the big three automobile manufacturers in Detroit has perpetuated the belief that only Controllers are effective, since the founder of the firm and his grandson both worked with a Controlling pattern. Any manager whose pattern causes discomfort to the entrenched management team is sent packing before he can prove his worth. Not even the founder's son, who was a quiet, introspective person, fit into the expectations of the organization long enough to have any lasting influence on it.

Other companies err in the other direction. A large wood and paper firm in Washington is managed by a team of close-knit Supporters who interact much as Roger does with his mining group. They're an amiable group of men who make their corporate decisions while golfing or cruising on the corporate yacht. Since they tend to see Controllers as rude, impatient boors, people with a more directive style are not welcome in the inner circle.

Several years ago the Washington firm acquired a Southern company that seemed to complement the parent firm's position in products and territories. On paper the merger looked perfect, but repeated conflicts arose when the Supporters of the parent company and the Controllers who had managed the Southern firm had to work closely together. Within a year the conflict was too great and many of the Controllers were forced to resign as the companies lost millions of dollars. The bitterness remains high among the Washington group, though they still have no idea why a merger, which seemed so good on paper when their lawyers were putting it together, failed so horrendously when the actual people involved tried to work in unison. A dozen key people in both firms were too far out in one of the personality-pattern sectors to work with people who had a very different pattern, and they were unwilling or unable to adapt.

Double Frustration

Most conflicts that are related to personality-pattern differences take place diagonally across the chart, with a Controller and a Supporter, or a Comprehender and an Entertainer, having the most trouble understanding and accepting each other. They have the most dissimilar traits, since Controllers and Entertainers share similar characteristics to the right of the line, while Controllers and Comprehenders share control above the horizontal line. Similarly, a Comprehender and a Supporter share cooperation, while a Supporter and an Entertainer share expression below the horizontal line. Conflict becomes more likely for anyone, regardless of his pattern, when he is forced from his comfort zone, since abrupt changes take place when a person is pushed beyond frustration and tension to stress.

A Controller who is pushed from his normal comfort zone by tension usually becomes autocratic, demanding that people do what he wants of them. If that behavior fails, however, and the tension becomes stress and deeper frustration, the Controller becomes an avoider in the relationship. His attempt to control the situation has failed and he cannot rationally find another approach to solving his problem. I watched this happen during a storm when I was grounded with many other passengers in an airport that was running short of room and comforts.

A burly man shouldered his way through the crowd to the ticket counter and commanded:

> Look here, boy. I *got* to get to El Paso right away. Put me on the *next* flight heading west of Kansas City.

When the soft-spoken Supporter agent told him that all flights west were booked and that many destinations were closed because of weather conditions, the large man became excited, shouting:

> Don't give me *that* crap! Just find one that's going my way and I'll transfer in Kansas City. But you get me on a flight *right now!*

The agent continued to explain, but he wasn't successful; the man became more frustrated and angry. Finally, when he realized that the agent's partner was calling airport security, and that he would not get on a plane regardless of how loudly he demanded his rights, he fired his last command and left. He said:

> I'm going to the bar and I'm going to sit there until you find me a flight and I'm going to bill all my drinks to your company. When you get that flight come and get me!

For all I know he is still seated there, for when he

stalked off I heard the quiet voice of the Supporter agent mutter to his partner:

The bastard'll be an alcoholic before *I* find a seat for him.

The Texan was consistent in his pattern, though he had become an avoider in doing so. Incidentally, Controllers are the people who create the most unnecessary tension and resentment among people with different styles. The frustrated Supporter saw the frustrated Controller as a bully, while the Controller felt the Supporter was incompetent for not fulfilling his commands.

A Supporter who is pushed from his comfort zone by frustration will usually yield on minor issues in order to preserve the relationship between himself and another person. If the tension increases enough to become stress, he abruptly shifts to mount an attack on the person or situation that is causing his frustration. This attack can be quite harmful to a person's ability to win support and cooperation, because it seems irrational. It looks out of character to a person who fails to realize that a cornered Supporter is like a cornered wolf, all teeth and claws, fighting for his life. Since the frustrating person did not behave "nicely" when the Supporter was so sincere, he has lost his right to decent treatment.

In the airport situation, the agent had been pressed beyond his comfort zone while he was still trying to explain that the weather took the decision out of his hands. When he was pushed still further, he attacked, though he did it quietly so as to keep his job. If the Controller had not yielded when he did, however, I fully expected the agent to try shoving the man's briefcase down his throat, just as "sincerely" as he tried to explain why he couldn't get him a seat to El Paso. If you are dealing with a smiling Supporter and discover that he is yielding to you, that is a good time to end your power play, for a little more stress may turn him into a raging attacker.

Here is an illustration that shows how the shifts can be expected to occur in a conflict between a Controller and a Supporter.

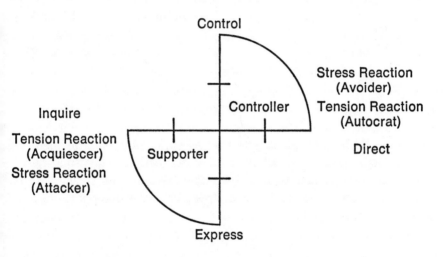

When an Entertainer is pushed from his comfort zone, his response is to attack to solve his problem. If that fails, he usually surrenders in a reversal of the Supporter's pattern of frustrated behavior. A Comprehender's tension response is to become an avoider and then an autocrat when the frustration becomes stressful. He will then make demands on a person that are not typical of his normal behavior, in a reversal of the Controller's pattern.

The second pattern reversal looks like this.

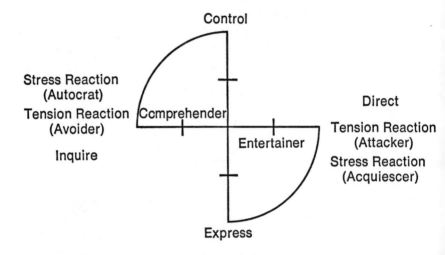

By learning these patterns and shifts, you can anticipate and predict the behavior of other people with amazing accuracy. You will also be able to anticipate what you will do under tension and stress, once you have identified your own pattern.

Identifying Your Own Pattern

Start by having four friends read Chapters Two and Three of this book. Then have them rank you according to how you cooperate or compete as compared to the rest of the people they know of your sex. Choose people to do this who are neither family members nor people who work for you *nor* people for whom you work on your job. People who are close to you may have insights into your true feelings that are deeper than your personality pattern. The same thing is likely to apply between a student and a teacher, or between a minister and a church member, so it is best to avoid such people with whom you have these kinds of relationships when selecting four peers to rate your pattern.

Instruct your four peers to indicate whether you are among the most cooperative, generally cooperative, generally competitive, or most competitive people they know. Supply each person with a horizontal and vertical scale like the one shown below. Have them, without consulting each other, locate your cooperative and competitive traits anywhere from zero to one hundred on the competitive scale. Instruct them not to put you on any one of the quarter points. If they want to place you at 50 percent, for example, they should place you at 51 percent instead.

Do the same with the vertical scale. Have the same four people rate you on degree of self-control or self-expression, in relation to the other people they know of your sex. Have them fill it out and return it to you.

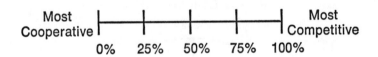

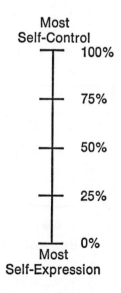

Add together the four scores you receive from *each* of the scales and divide the sums by four to get an average you will plot in the figure below. You will plot the horizontal score on the Direct/Inquire scale and the vertical score on the Control/Express line. Draw a perpendicular line from each average score until they intersect in one of the four sectors to indicate the personality pattern your peers see you using regularly. If either of the average scores falls directly on a line, add two points to it before plotting it on the chart. After you have determined your own pattern, you can use the knowledge you gained by identifying the patterns of others and then predicting their needs and behavior.

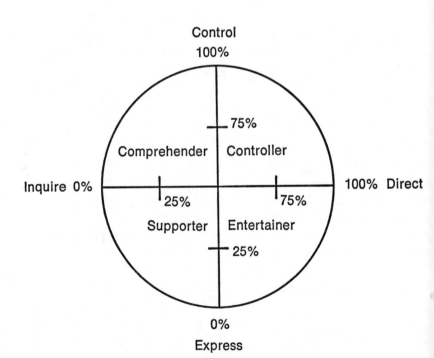

Be careful not to decide upon a person's pattern when he is out of his comfort zone, or your tactics will be useless when he returns to his normal manner of relating to others. That would be like using a faulty thermometer to check someone's temperature. Of course, there is not much point in trying to interpret someone's pattern and predict his behavior unless you are comfortable yourself. Otherwise, much of his behavior may be a reaction to your own and will thus be invalid when you return to normal.

Identifying Controllers

Remember that a Controller is a person who is most comfortable as he uses emotional self-control and directs people what to do. He is most comfortable when he feels in control of situations and people who could force him from his comfort zone. He also prefers working toward practical achievements and speaking frankly about issues that affect him personally. Your goal is to help him remain in his comfort zone so he will accept you and your concepts while you negotiate successfully with the techniques taught in Parts Two and Three of *Nice Guys Finish First*. Here are some searching questions you can ask a mutual acquaintance before you meet for the first time someone whose pattern you have not yet established.

> Do you feel that Dan is more comfortable working with ideas or solving practical problems? (Controllers prefer solving practical problems to dealing with abstract ideas.)
>
> Does he seem more comfortable telling anecdotes, or does he prefer giving direct instructions to people? (Controllers prefer telling others what to do directly rather than with innuendos.)
>
> When you visit Dan to discuss a critical issue, do you find that he prefers getting right to business, or does he like to chat for a while? (Controllers prefer a fast approach to problems, while relating comes later, if at all.)

Does Dan make immediate decisions, or does he habitually look for more information before he makes up his mind? (Controllers choose rapidly, often working from a bare outline of facts.)

Is Dan task oriented or people oriented? Why? (Controllers are definitely task oriented.)

In many cases a person's office, room, workspace, or manner of dressing will give the clues you need to make up your mind about his pattern. This is not always true in business offices, of course, for some companies have strict regulations about furniture, decorations, and dress that squelch individual differences. For example, a large computer company even had a date when the men could switch from long-sleeve white shirts to short-sleeve white shirts. And woe to any man foolish enough to change before the sanctioned date, to say nothing of wearing colored shirts or flamboyant ties or jackets!

A Controller's room or office will usually reflect a no-nonsense view of efficiency, with tasks rather than people uppermost in mind. Since he needs to feel in control, his materials and furniture may look like they were arranged by an efficiency expert. His desk may be bare except for the one item he is working on, or it may have several stacks of paper arranged to be easily reached. The desk will certainly be the bridge of his ship, with the telephone, calculator, and writing instruments conveniently placed within arm's length. His desk may be a barrier behind which he maintains his sense of personal power over those who enter his domain. A spartan decor is often a command not to linger too long, as the entire motif conveys his desire for you to speak right up, say your piece, accept his Controller's rapid decisions, and leave quietly without further questions.

If you are still in doubt about a person's pattern, here are some questions you can use to generate clues during your visit. They should be asked with discretion and sensitivity, of course, rather than blurted out because you are not able to become comfortable with him.

> Could you give me a short summary of your job/life/interests here?
>
> Do you find the theoretical aspects of chemistry/psychology/marketing most challenging to you, or the practical application of what you know?
>
> What bothers you the most about your children/employees/peers as you deal with them?
>
> How do you get people to do what needs to be done?

If your clues reveal a person who deals in no-nonsense practical issues, enjoys using power openly, is reserved in his mannerisms and dress, and is not particularly interested in adjusting to the views of others, he is most likely a Controller. For a final check ask yourself whether this person often has an expressionless face, has an unchanging voice, and uses few gestures. If so, expect that he will tell others what to do, make demands if he has the power, want to solve problems practically, and become impatient with concern about too many details. Under tension he will make autocratic demands, but under stress, when he feels like he is losing control of a situation, he will often flee the scene as an avoider.

Identifying Entertainers

An Entertainer is a person who is direct in his relationships, expressing his feelings openly and frequently. The five questions given in the section on Controllers can also be used to identify Entertainers. If you have an opportunity to do so, ask them of a person who knows the man or woman you are going to deal with.

> Do you feel that Jean is more comfortable working with ideas or solving practical problems? (Entertainers prefer grand sweeping ideas to the routine of putting them into practice.)

Does she seem more comfortable telling anecdotes, or does she prefer giving direct instructions to people? (Entertainers prefer using stories and jokes when making a point or giving instructions.)

When you visit Jean to discuss a critical issue, do you find that she prefers getting right to business, or does she like to chat for a while? (Entertainers prefer socializing and dealing with emotions before getting to work.)

Does Jean make immediate decisions, or does she habitually look for more information before she makes up her mind? (Entertainers choose rapidly, often before they have the information they really need for a total picture.)

Is Jean task oriented or people oriented? Why? (Entertainers are definitely people oriented.)

An Entertainer's office or room will usually have a people-oriented motif. There will frequently be plaques, posters, mottoes, and photographs of people the entertainer admires. The desk may appear disorganized or even cluttered with things that have no relationship to his work, and the furniture will reflect his desire to be with people rather than doing tasks per se, since he feels that no tasks will be completed without inspiring the employees, students, or children.

One executive I know quite well doesn't even have a desk, but a round table surrounded by low chairs. In the corners of the room are the papers and books he needs. The walls are covered with mementos from his career, his athletic achievements, and past relationships. It is obvious that an Entertainer like himself uses his pattern effectively, for the decor invites people to sit down, be at ease, and tell him what's important to the relationship.

An Entertainer's movements are broad and his clothes are colorful much of the time. He is frequently considered an expansive, talkative personality whose individuality is obvious. An Entertainer will frequently pull his chair close to yours and use his hands and facial expression to convey his message and to emphasize his points. His voice is a tool that expresses his emotions almost as soon as he experiences them. If you need more clues, you can ask the same questions given in the preceding section.

Could you give me a short summary of your job/life/interests here?

Do you find the theoretical aspects of chemistry/psychology/marketing most challenging to you, or the practical application of what you know?

What bothers you the most about your children/employees/peers as you deal with them?

How do you get people to do what needs to be done?

If your clues reveal a person who deals in "big pictures" without thinking through the details, who has vast dreams that may never come true, who is fashionable or modish in dress, fast spoken, and uses mobile facial expressions and gestures, he is most likely an Entertainer. Expect that he will soon tell you what he feels, turn you on with his ideas, or become bored if you linger too long on facts or figures without applying them to people. Under tension he will become an attacker, and under stress he will acquiesce in surrender.

Identifying Supporters

A Supporter combines expression with inquiry, appearing instantly to care deeply about the people he meets. He or she is interested in feelings, both yours and his, though he is less likely to speak about them than an Entertainer to the right of the pattern chart. To gain more information ask the following questions of a mutual friend.

Do you feel that Alvin is more comfortable working with ideas or solving practical problems? (Supporters prefer working with abstract ideas that are indirectly related to people.)

Does he seem more comfortable telling anecdotes or does

he prefer giving direct instructions to people? (Supporters avoid giving direct instruction, often veiling their suggestions or commands in anecdotes and illustrations.)

When you visit Alvin to discuss a critical issue, do you find that he prefers getting right to business or does he like to chat for a while? (Supporters prefer making other people comfortable before getting to work.)

Does Alvin make immediate decisions or does he habitually look for more information before he makes up his mind? (Supporters often want plenty of data so that they will be safe, and frequently choose because someone has won their trust by being supportive.)

Is he task oriented or people oriented? (Supporters are definitely people oriented.)

The decor of a Supporter's office or room is open and friendly. It may have flowers or photographs of family and friends. The desk may be cluttered or it may be neatly arranged, but it is likely to be placed in such a way that he can swing away from his work to relate to visitors with no barrier between them. Visitors will often be encouraged to become comfortable for a nice chat by the soft furniture. I once had a Supporting editor working for me who was so gifted that he had nothing to do at times. He soon arranged his office so as to prevent me from seeing that he was writing material of his own. Since business was slow at the time, I told him that I didn't care whether he did that, as long as my materials received his excellent, fast work. In a few days his office was rearranged in a manner more appropriate to his personality pattern.

You can ask the following questions to gain additional clues.

Could you give me a short summary of your job/life/interests here?

Do you find the theoretical aspects of chemistry/psychology/marketing most challenging to you, or the practical application of what you know?

What bothers you the most about your children/employees/
peers as you deal with them?

How do you get people to do what needs to be done?

If your clues reveal that the person is one who seems
quite sincere and open in relationships, who wants to help
you achieve your goals, who is casual in dress, and who is
accepting in his words and movements, he is most likely
a Supporter. Keep in mind that he may continue to accept
you personally even after he has decided not to do what
you want him to. You may have to probe to find this out,
for he will continue to be nice and may even acquiesce to
your demands if the stakes are not too great. If the frustrations grow worse, however, he may well become an attacker, to your surprise.

Identifying Comprehenders

A Comprehender combines cooperation and self-control
much as does Viking football coach Bud Grant, who is
often chided by sportscasters for his expressionless manner
whether he is winning or losing. The questions you can
ask a mutual friend are the same, but you should be looking for a different set of answers.

Do you feel that Dianne is more comfortable working with
ideas or solving practical problems? (Comprehenders prefer
working with abstract ideas and facts rather than with people.)

Does she seem more comfortable telling anecdotes or does
she prefer giving direct instructions to people? (Comprehenders seldom use stories or jokes, but prefer giving factual
instructions.)

When you visit Dianne to discuss a critical issue, do you
find that she prefers getting right to business or does she like
to chat for a while? (Comprehenders rarely will chat with
strangers without dealing with factual matters first.)

Does Dianne make immediate decisions or does she habitually look for more information before she makes up her
mind? (Comprehenders habitually look for as much data as

they can possibly find on any given subject, so their decisions are often late in the game.)

Is she task oriented or people oriented? Why? (Comprehenders are definitely task oriented.)

The most frequent climate of a Comprehender's office or room is that of someone with a well-ordered intellect who is constantly seeking information, but resisting decisions until he is certain of all the facts. If anything is hanging on the wall it is probably a diploma or a chart of some kind. There will be few personal photographs present, but often a cheap reproduction of a painting, because he or she has learned that other people expect it. It may be dusty or hanging askew because he hasn't looked at it for months. There may be many books of a technical nature rather than biographical or inspirational works.

The furniture and its arrangement will reflect a need to keep a proper distance from visitors, who may be seen as intruders who are consuming time that could be better spent on collecting data for doing *real* work. There frequently seems to be a place for everything, with everything in its place. In fact, this could be the Comprehender's life motto. He will resist dealing with new problems and relationships until the one project he is currently working on has been resolved. Since he usually wants more data, obtaining it may take more time than you can afford to let him have, to the distress of Controllers and Entertainers, who expect quick and simple solutions to life's demands. His mannerisms and clothing may be conservative, while his facial expressions will be immobile as he talks to you. Under tension he will avoid situations that trouble him; under stress he will often become autocratic.

To create more clues you can ask the following questions.

Could you give me a short summary of your job/life/interests here?

Do you find the theoretical aspects of chemistry/psychology/marketing most challenging to you, or the practical application of what you know?

What bothers you the most about your children/employees/peers as you deal with them?

How do you get people to do what needs to be done?

If your clues reveal a fact-oriented person who wants things to be correct at all times, who is reserved in his relationships, reluctant to assume the trappings of power, conservative in his manners and dress, even-spoken to the point of boredom, and secretive about his feelings, he is most likely a Comprehender.

Applying Knowledge

To influence a Controller, support his conclusions and give him options so he will feel in control as he makes his choices. Keep most of your feelings to yourself, stay on schedule, and be on time for meetings—neither early nor late. Don't discuss your intuitive decisions, but wrap them in facts. Don't waste his time socializing, but get right to the point unless he reveals his desire to chat as he relaxes after a task is complete. Being efficient reveals your "true" character to a Controller.

To influence an Entertainer, support his dreams and ambitions as you offer him stimulating ideas. Use technical data sparingly, but supply professional opinions from people who impress him. Don't make the mistake of dwelling too long on details, but quickly move to the interpersonal advantages that cooperating with you will bring. Keep things moving along at a good pace so he can be swept up in the ideas that make him feel good. Always be stimulating and ready for a joke or a laugh. But be sure to get a commitment of time and goals from him before investing time or money in his plans. He does become bored quickly.

To influence a Supporter, show a sincere interest in his

feelings as a person by finding an area of common interest such as hobbies, hometowns, jobs, or so on. Demonstrate that happy, peaceful relationships are important to you by sharing your emotions and ideas. Give him adequate assurances and guarantees as you remain casual and trustworthy. Don't offer many options or press for too rapid a decision. Options are often seen as ultimatums, particularly when they come from a Controller, who doesn't understand the importance of relating to a man or a woman with this pattern. Always be sincere, for that is the key to persuading a Supporter.

To influence a Comprehender, take your time, but be gently persistent when he is under tension or he will avoid you. On the other hand, if you don't press some, he may do nothing at all but look for more information. Give him data and summaries that have no contradictions in them: conflicting facts quickly alarm him. Make an original contribution to his plans in a logical and unemotional manner. Remain serious as you communicate. Too many options will overwhelm him, for he will want to think through them all before choosing one. Be somewhat formal, avoid chattiness, and don't be clever with words or ideas. Let your acts be "correct" with a Comprehender, for he wants certainty more than do people with other personality patterns.

Remember that you cannot avoid using your pattern for long without creating tension for yourself. Therefore, don't put on an elaborate act, since your nonverbal communication would give you away. Simply make the effort to slip into his frame of reference long enough for him to accept you rather than becoming defensive because your pattern displeases him. After rapport has been established and you focus on working, playing, or living together without stress, you will slip back into your own pattern unconsciously, but he will very likely have accepted that you are a competent person, even though he may never realize why he feels that way about you.

The closer you are to the edge of the chart, the harder it will be for you to shift for a while. The closer to the middle, the easier the shift, of course. The opposite is true also. You will have to work harder to win rapport with people whose patterns are closer to the edge if they are in a different sector from you, but it can be done, except with people like Lombardi, who are so close to the edge that they cannot imagine why anyone would be different from themselves.

The Personality-Pattern Organizer shown on the following page summarizes the crucial traits that will help you identify a person's pattern as well as telling you how to behave as a means of establishing rapport. Identifying traits are outside the circle, while your choices are on the inside.

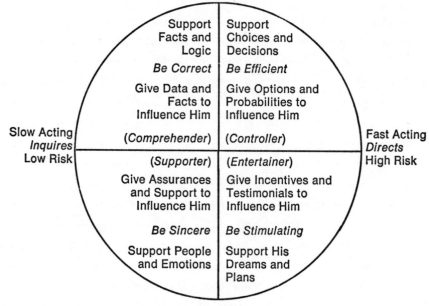

Cool/Distant
Precise About the Use of Time
Wants Facts and Figures
Controls

Support Facts and Logic

Be Correct

Give Data and Facts to Influence Him

(Comprehender)

Support Choices and Decisions

Be Efficient

Give Options and Probabilities to Influence Him

(Controller)

(Supporter)

Give Assurances and Support to Influence Him

Be Sincere

Support People and Emotions

(Entertainer)

Give Incentives and Testimonials to Influence Him

Be Stimulating

Support His Dreams and Plans

Slow Acting
Inquires
Low Risk

Fast Acting
Directs
High Risk

Expresses
Wants Feelings and Concern
Imprecise About the Use of Time
Warm/Close

CHAPTER FOUR

Communicating
to Lead

Few of the people with whom you successfully negotiate will know anything about personality patterns or how quickly they respond to appropriate payoffs. Even fewer of them will realize how powerful an influence the unconscious workings of the mind have on their decisions. They only know that they like some people and dislike others, without really knowing why. They have some vague idea that there may be valid reasons, but most of them are fabricated to explain their feelings rather than based on real facts.

Most people still believe the Victorian myth that men and women proceed logically while making decisions based on facts they have learned. Controllers and Comprehenders are especially prone to assume that they are cool and logical, but under the personality patterns they use, they are like everyone else. They fail to realize that men and women usually do what another person asks of them for highly emotional reasons. And since people fear the unknown, they generally find a "logical" reason by which they prove to themselves that their acts are based on facts rather than on feelings. It is with this deep, frequently illogical sphere

83

of emotions that a negotiator must cope if he expects to be consistently successful.

Freud put an end to the myth of human rationality and logic within the medical and psychological professions, but for the most part his discoveries have not been accepted by men and women. They automatically react to what you do and say according to their unconscious feelings and then believe that they have thought through the ramifications of their choices. Interpersonal conflicts usually occur when two people are competing for the same thing, when they are forced out of their comfort zone, or when unconscious emotions dominate their actions. And when men or women realize that other people act illogically, they nevertheless continue to assume that their own actions are somehow logical and based on facts.

Each person evaluates his situations or decisions by filtering new information through a perceptual-screening process whose purpose is to protect his ego from self-devaluation or confusing new ideas. If a new concept allows him to remain comfortable according to the personal reality he learned in childhood, he accepts it. If he does not, such as when people of another race or religion move out of the roles he assigned to them earlier, he rejects the new information as being incorrect.

Not long ago an elderly white man told me that blacks are less intelligent than whites because they have small heads, which contain less brain matter than those of "real people." He went on to say that blacks also have wide flaring nostrils that enable them to breathe more deeply and thus to work harder than white people. That, he said, was why black athletes do so well in professional sports. When I protested that he was talking about some of the Central African people of the Congo having smaller heads —which has nothing to do with brain capacity, however— he denied it. When I said that Africans from other localities have large heads and aquiline features, he disagreed. A few days later I showed him a book of photographs of the Masai, Zulu, and Ethiopian peoples, which demonstrated conclusively that they do not have small heads and large noses. He looked at them for a moment and then said:

> They're not *really* Negroes. They must have enough white blood to change their characteristics. Real Negroes have small heads, can't think well, and have big noses so they can work harder than regular people do.

I don't know what frightened him so badly in childhood that he has been unable to accept blacks as completely human, but nothing I could demonstrate with photographs, medical research, or religious values was going to get through his perceptual screen, which was fixed to filter out anything that would disturb the reality he had accepted since childhood. But something of deep emotional significance did occur around the turn of the century to hurt him, for the man has as small a head as I have ever seen on an adult male.

Nonverbal Communication

On the surface, interpersonal communication seems simple enough. All you should have to do is tell another person what you want him to know or how you feel about a given situation. People normally do this without realizing what others are actually perceiving or how they interpret what is being said, unless the other person is obviously out of his comfort zone. Effective communication, which leads to commitment, is much more complex than that, however.

According to research done by Wilson, no more than 7 percent of what a person communicates is put into words. About 38 percent is reflected in body language, while about

55 percent is transmitted through the tone of voice. Each person learns to interpret nonverbal communication from his mother, before he learns to understand or use words. Every young mother soon learns that her infant rests more comfortably in her arms when she is happy than he does when she is angry or tense. The child has learned to react to the tone of her voice and the tenseness of her muscles, and this continues with such influence that only 7 percent of what we communicate is actually put into words.

Not long ago I was talking to a blind friend as our wives chatted for a moment and then wandered away. After a while Ron turned to me and asked where the women had gone. Without thinking, I nodded my head toward them and said, "Over there." Ron repeated his question and I made the same unthinking response, but automatically expanded it to say, "Standing over there," gesturing with my hand. After his third try at getting an answer *he* could interpret, I realized that my nonverbal communication was not going to help very much and told him that they had gone into the patio to look at our host's flowers. Only then did he understand what my body language couldn't tell him, though he would have interpreted my tone of voice quickly enough if I had become annoyed by his questions and allowed my impatience to creep into my voice.

This use of nonverbal communication takes place all the time, and people unconsciously respond without thinking about why. Imagine that you are in your office, working on some papers, when your boss enters, speaking in a conversational tone. His face is composed and his body is relaxed as he says, "What are you doing?" Following the Law of Reciprocity you will probably tell him about your task without any tension, replying in the same manner.

If he entered your office, planted both fists in the middle of your desk and demanded sharply, "What *are* you doing?" you would certainly feel some apprehension and wonder what had gone wrong to force him from his comfort zone.

If, however, he leaned over your desk, put clenched fists on your papers and shouted in your face, *"What are you doing?"* you would know that you were in trouble and had better find out what you could do to get things back to normal once more. He would have your complete attention until the problem was solved. Yet in each case the same words were used. Only the tone of voice and body language were different. When this happens to you, you interpret the changes very carefully. But when you are talking to someone you are not nearly as careful. This is the reason why so many interpersonal failures occur.

If your manager had leaned over you, clenched his fists and planted them on your desk, and then spoken softly or denied that he was angry, you might have become confused by the conflicting messages being sent, since people are so acutely aware of such contradictions when they affect their well-being. People have learned that a contradiction between verbal and nonverbal messages is likely an effort to deceive, or else the speaker is losing control of his emotions and acting irrationally. Either interpretation produces a reluctance to become vulnerable to him. Obviously, if you do this when you communicate with others, they will interpret your acts as illogical or deceitful and therefore it will be that much harder for you to reach your goals.

Authentic Communication

Dr. Carl Rogers, from the Western Behavioral Sciences Institute, wrote that each person must remain "authentic" as he deals with other people. By that he means that you must be emotionally honest enough to recognize what you are feeling at a given time, accept your emotions as normal and legitimate under the circumstances, and be willing to express your feelings in a supportive way when doing so is appropriate.

As I said in the preceding chapter, the people who have the most trouble sharing their feelings, even when they personally understand and accept them, are the Controllers and Comprehenders at the top half of the chart. They frequently avoid telling others what they feel when it would increase their effectiveness to do so. Of course, Entertainers and Supporters often make mistakes in the opposite manner, telling what they feel when it is not appropriate for them to do so, thus alienating the people they need commitment from. Fortunately, there is a happy medium between these two extremes that you can follow to increase your interpersonal skills.

Men and women frequently have good reasons for concealing their feelings, however, unless they have learned to communicate authentically without driving the listener from his comfort zone. When a parent demands that a long-neglected lawn be mowed before the car can be used on a Friday date, total honesty about a person's feelings can lead to interpersonal disaster and a collapse of real communication between parent and child. Fortunately, a perceptive person can learn several ways of communicating without damaging the egos of the parties involved. The techniques taught in the chapter on conflict management enable people to understand each other and to remain accepting even when specific demands cannot be met. Both parties are able to express their feelings without having to bottle up the resentment until it explodes and cruel words, which are much more difficult to retract than body language, are spoken.

Unfortunately our society teaches people to control their acts without showing them how to understand the emotions that cause the behavior. Probably not one parent in a hundred teaches his kids that all emotions are normal and have survival value. Most adults want their children to feel ambition and love, but they become anxious when youngsters express fear, anger, or sexual desire. Yet, in appropriate situations, those unwanted feelings are not only normal, they enable a person to survive more effectively as a human.

When communicating authentically, it helps to realize that in periods of uncertainty, such as getting acquainted or dealing with someone new who has authority or power over you, it is normal to try to discover how the other is going to respond before you blurt out your opinions, problems, or demands. Every doctor or psychologist has people come to him with a story about a "friend" who needs help, only to admit, as the strangeness of the situation abates, that he is really the one needing counseling. Since people do this to keep from getting hurt, they may never get around to discussing problems openly if the other person doesn't demonstrate his willingness to accept them without judging or devaluing their feelings. Leonard Jackson told how this happened to one of his students in junior high school.

Leonard is a science and math instructor in the Atlanta school system who came to class one morning to find his principal and an eighth-grade girl awaiting him. As the girl looked around the room, she turned to him and said, "Who did that awful poster over there?" The principal immediately bristled, but Leonard, who understands that people often start important conversations by protecting themselves, laughed and answered, "Around here we ask only that you do the best you can on your projects. I don't expect you to be Picasso."

Then the girl pointed to some charts on the board to say, "Can anyone in your classes really use that stuff?" Again the principal grunted sarcastically and said that since she was new she didn't know what she was talking about. But

Leonard shrugged and replied, "Not everyone, but some can. Those who cannot are learning, and I'll be happy to explain it to you if you like."

Then the girl seemed at ease, for the teacher had realized what she really wanted to know, even if the principal did not. The new student had learned what quality of work was acceptable to the teacher and how he would react when he found out that math was rather fuzzy to her; and, more important at the time, she had not become vulnerable by asking the questions directly. As they got her some books and assigned her a table, the girl talked to him about various things, but never spoke to the principal again. She had learned who would help her and who would not understand what it was like to be a new kid in school. The principal didn't understand why he had been ignored by the two, but then, as a blunderer who has no idea of the importance of emotions, he is usually excluded from acceptance by many of the students and teachers.

Communicating Crucial Answers

Frequently, when a person fails to realize that someone is testing him, he thinks an agreement has been reached when the other person has only grown quiet because he wants to avoid a confrontation. One mother told me:

> I try to be logical, but it blows up in my face. The kids never listen until I demand that they do as I want. They never seem to hear me until I become angry.

Children, students, employees, spouses, and peers avoid authentic communication for a number of reasons. First of all, people resent being manipulated or criticized, especially if they feel they are being denied their legitimate payoff in the relationship. They dislike being lectured, talked down to, or criticized, though they will tolerate these things if some of the payoffs remain great enough to compensate for them. For example, the owner of a certain major manufacturing firm is a self-made man with a limited education. And though he is a sadistic bully who enjoys humiliating his educated executives in order to feel better about his lack of education, he pays them enough money so that they continue working for him until they find a less painful president to work for. Then they leave, helping account for the firm's terrible turnover rate, but confirming the owner's perception that he is being taken advantage of by a group of ungrateful wretches who have no loyalty. He passes all information through his perceptual screen, and it all comes out right to make him feel better about his resentment.

Often men and women fail to engage in useful conversations when they are in conflict across the personality patterns. This is frequent when each of two people is trying to remain in his comfort zone regardless of what happens in the relationship.

Anyone who has listened to conversations between frustrated people is amazed at how frequently each person ignores what the other is trying to communicate. The conversation sounds like two audio tapes made in advance and played at the same time, without any knowledge of what the other person is going to say. One monologue consists of criticisms, instructions, and admonitions, while the parallel recording is filled with defenses, denials, and rejection of responsibility.

Such a conversation reveals that the critical person is attempting to use power to demand compliance, as well as failing to understand how people can resolve difficulties and negotiate solutions or compromises. After all, few things will ever be resolved if both people are determined to have all the winnings.

The approach to successful personal communication that I advocate in this chapter is based on the fact that the

vast majority of men and women really do prefer interpersonal rewards to deprivation, respect to humiliation,
and praise to criticism. The engineering manager in one
huge electrical generating complex told me how he used
these concepts effectively. He had put his construction crew
on a rush job to pour some concrete footing for a special
building and then had been forced to pull them off abruptly
when the Atomic Energy Commission needed additional
power for some confidential experiments being conducted
nearby. Donald realized that stopping the job of pouring on
such short notice without an explanation to his foreman
was likely to produce resentment and resistance. Therefore
he approached the hardworking but rigid Comprehender in
a carefully thought-out manner.

He didn't trigger resentment by impatiently saying something like:

> Dammit, Andy. Accept the fact that I sometimes know things
> you don't, and do as you're told. Put number eleven boiler on
> line, because I need it;
> or,
> You're too compulsive, and have to become more flexible;
> or,
> It's not my fault I didn't get the word any sooner. Blame them
> upstairs.

Instead Donald thought for a moment and realized that
Andy had worked hard all week to get the forms in place
in spite of the tight schedule. He realized that Andy hated
surprises and was impatient about being prodded too fast
when he had to think issues and ramifications through to his
satisfaction. The superintendent thought that he had better
take time to show Andy how much he appreciated his extra
effort and that he understood his emotions even if Andy
hid them beneath his Comprehender exterior. To the foreman he approached it like this:

> *Donald*: Let's go get a cup of coffee. I'm run ragged from those forms this past week.

When the men were seated drinking their coffee, he continued by saying:

> *Donald*: You seem unhappy that we can't finish the foundations this week like we planned.
> *Andy*: I sure am!
> *Donald*: You put so much work into meeting my schedule, didn't you?
> *Andy*: That's right. We all worked like hell to get them ready for pouring.
> *Donald*: And I come along to pull the rug from under you, and the boys, to tell you to repair a boiler we haven't used in three months. It sounds crazy, doesn't it?
> *Andy*: You said it!

Donald shook his head and shrugged as he made a nonverbal expression of acceptance as the two men continued drinking their coffee, but he didn't try to defend himself or try to explain his reasons. He simply remained accepting of Andy from his comfort zone and allowed Andy to return to his. Finally the foreman spoke again.

> *Andy*: But I gotta admit that you never promised to make sense all the time when you hired me. I know you too well to think you did this without a good reason. You must know what you're doing. Let me go fix your rusty old kettle for you.

Andy's tension was gone, removed by Donald's acceptance of his resentment without responding in a critical manner. Andy was hooked according to the Law of Reciprocity, because Donald knew what he was doing. Andy and the crew worked at full speed the rest of the day as he encouraged the men to keep them moving along. Previously, when Andy had been forced from his comfort zone, he had made life miserable with his nit-picking attention to detail. Sooner or later he found something to his dislike and became autocratic. Naturally, when their boss was angry, the men spent more time and effort protecting themselves than they did offering him their commitment, until everyone had a chance to sleep off the frustrations. On that day, Donald told me, the few minutes he spent with Andy changed the entire climate of the crew.

When a person is frustrated, frightened, or angry, his ability to reason and communicate is severely handicapped. A frustrated worker, student, or spouse will not accept correction or advice as easily as he will when he is in his comfort zone. Not only that, the frustrated person wants everyone to understand him and to adjust to his needs and emotions at the time. He is so caught up in his own needs that he doesn't think of explaining his feelings to a tormentor; he may even shed his veneer of civilized behavior to react on a primitive, gut level. Ten minutes earlier he may not have done that and he may not ten minutes later, but he cannot accept accusations or criticisms forced upon him at that time of frustration.

Adversary Relationships

I wrote that few people are ever taught in childhood to deal with their emotions effectively; even fewer learn how to use feelings to win when they want to. For example, parents frequently force their children to pretend that they don't really feel what they do. When a child shouts at his mother, "I hate you!" the mother frequently does one of two things. Either she punishes the child for telling the truth, or else she "reasons" with him, telling him that nice people don't actually feel such emotions, that what he feels is only a mild dislike rather than rage.

In the first case the child learns to live by the Law of the Jungle, hiding his real feelings from the people who control him and acting out his angers when he reaches a place of control. The whole idea of sharing the winnings in life is foreign to him. In the second example, the child learns to go through life doing what he pleases and then denying that he is responsible. He never comes to grips with his emotions, especially the primordial angers that lurk in the mind. How can he be assaulting others with those angers, when he is such a nice person? Any disturbing information is filtered away by his perceptual screen, which always makes things come out right for himself. He doesn't ever become authentic with others.

In one of the schools where I taught, I had a problem child in my homeroom—a beautiful youngster who had every advantage except a mother who could face reality. Every time Carl got into trouble his mother found a way to pin the blame on me, the principal, other kids, or the school system. One afternoon matters came to a head when I found him pummeling the least likely boy in the class, one who had been reared to treat others fairly. When I pulled them apart I yelled, "Who started this?"

Without blinking an eye Carl looked right at me and said, "It started when he *hit me back!*" Obviously such a neat kid as himself couldn't be blamed for doing something wrong. It is equally obvious that many people do the same thing well into adult life and then cannot understand why they are ostracized by everyone who doesn't like pulling their chestnuts from the fire. When the members of a family or any other group start using self-deception to feel better about themselves, an adversary relationship is virtually inevitable. Both people or groups start interpreting their acts in the very best possible light, and those of the adversaries in the worst possible way.

Unless you anticipate the resentment and anger that thoughtless or self-serving words arouse in people, you can very quickly develop more adversaries than you can placate. And adversaries will go to great lengths to keep you a loser. They will do so because they find greater satisfaction in defeating you, even if they lose themselves, than in allowing you to take the prizes of life, because they feel they are getting the short end of the stick anyway. Beating you out of the reward if they do not get it themselves isn't logical, but it does make them feel better for a while.

Once an adversary relationship has been created, everyone becomes a loser. Edward Daniels had run his large, city school as his personal kingdom for ten years as principal. Then the housing patterns changed with the construction of freeways and a federal judge ordered busing to achieve racial balance for the student population. Under pressure from different minority groups, several black teachers, two Mexican-Americans, and one Native American teacher were assigned to the school over Daniels' protests. He struggled futilely against the new reality until his beleaguered heart faltered.

Daniels was a no-nonsense Controller of the tell-'em-what school of administration. He called it majoring in the fundamentals, but his prime motivation was to keep himself from becoming anxious with people he did not understand. He found that expressing his hostilities by insulting teachers and students made him feel better. He rationalized his attacks by saying that his methods motivated people to do their best.

As the community and the school changed, his style of leadership became less and less effective, so he resorted to the only concepts he admitted through his perceptual screen. He started telling people, including reporters, that the problems in his school were caused by the minority students and teachers, who didn't really want an education. He tried to tighten up his control on the faculty and the student body, but succeeded only in developing a critical adversary relationship. He no longer had the power to demand compliance, but he pretended to himself that he did.

Within a year after the beginning of busing, parents had him in court for insulting students; the minority teachers demanded an investigation, alleging that he had misused federal funds; and the students had fire-bombed his car twice. His heart failed and he had to accept a medical retirement, though he had told me on several occasions that he was going to become the superintendent of a city system somewhere and he didn't care what he had to do to reach his goal. He is a bitter and frustrated man who putters a lot in his rose garden, but it hardly compensates for the loss of usefulness he caused himself by creating an adversary relationship that destroyed his life's work. Only by changing his perception of life and by winning cooperation could he have reached his goal, but because of his attitudes about nonwhite people he could not do these things.

Three Alternatives

As I look at my own experiences and read what I can from psychology, I find only three alternatives of leadership open to anyone who wants to lead other people successfully. They are:

> Authoritarian Leadership
> Laissez-faire Leadership
> Basic-Principle Leadership

You can try to be a drill master whose energy is wasted as Daniels' was—spending your time outwitting the people whose commitment you need, despite the fact that all normal people want to feel good about themselves, to be useful, and to enjoy their relationships. But the outcome of such an authoritarian approach is clearly visible in one's future. The people around you will lose, and so will you, if you are determined to leave the game with all the chips. Herzberg called this the Kick in the Arse school of leadership, and no one has really made it work since Genghis Khan—but then his army was bigger than yours. It is a doomed, self-defeating approach to winning, for you need the approval of your spouse, children, friends, peers, and employees to become a winner, as well as approval from your investment counselor.

The second alternative open to each person is somewhat

less painful to the people around you, but it doesn't produce any more victories for everyone concerned than the first alternative. It is the *Laissez-faire* method of winning commitment, in which the people you want to influence are allowed or even encouraged to do their own thing with total freedom. On the surface this would seem to open the springs of creativity, but that is not the case. Few groups, regardless of their size, work well together unless their activities are well planned and coordinated. During the sixties, many youth communes were organized with the idea that each person would do his own thing and perfect happiness and contentment would result. What actually happened was that much music was played and few crops were cultivated If it had not been for food stamps and welfare payments the free spirits would have starved in short order. Laissez-faire leadership is actually an abdication of personal responsibility in any leadership role. It confuses people who need structure and neglects organization of duties. We have seen the disastrous results among the street children of our inner cities whose parents are so busy trying to survive financially or are so psychologically inept that the youngsters are left leaderless much of the time.

The third approach is to consistently communicate and reinforce the Basic Principle when dealing with other people, that *good things happen to people who cooperate*. It uses the concepts taught in *Nice Guys Finish First* to convey the message that the men and women who work with you will find greater rewards in doing so than in ignoring you or working as an adversary. To offer the payoffs consistently, you organize your requirements and rewards in such a way that people receive physical, psychological, and spiritual payoffs because of the kind of person you are.

Nothing demonstrates the effectiveness of the Basic Principle approach any better than the research conducted by Lewin. He used three work/play groups of preadolescent boys. Each of the three group leaders was working under instructions from Lewin. The first leader was instructed to be Authoritarian, the second to be Laissez-faire, and the third to use the Basic Principle approach, though Lewin called them by different names.

There was little doubt that the boys in the Authoritarian group worked harder and faster as long as the leader remained beside them, ready to criticize, select goals for the lads, and to drive them on. But when he moved away, the work slackened at once. When he left the room, chaos erupted. The boys, evidently frustrated by being manipulated, broke each other's projects, hid tools, and got into fights regularly. They had been treated as hoodlums and, following the Law of Reciprocity, they became hoodlums as soon as they had an opportunity. They were almost immediately converted into adversaries.

The Laissez-faire group met with a leader who offered no suggestions, made no attempt to organize the projects, and made no corrections when the boys made a mistake on their projects. The activities were never completed, though there was some creative horseplay. The boys didn't even select a leader of their own as the boys would have done on the playground, because the adult was present, but not functioning as a leader. Really, very little happened one way or another.

The last group, the one that used an interpersonal rewards system, was organized and assisted by the adult leader. It had by far the best experience. The adult didn't try to manipulate the boys, but served as a resource person who helped them negotiate the use of tools and equipment, select appropriate projects, and advise them when they had problems. The third group of boys did almost as much work as the Authoritarian group when the leader was present. But unlike that group, which fell apart when the leader was absent, the Basic Principle group continued to work as well when their leader left the room. Once the

boys had participated in selecting their projects and received the adult's help when they needed it, the tasks
became theirs instead of his, so they kept working for the
payoff of completing them, rather than destroying the
projects for the sake of frustrating an adversary. They were
winning their rewards and they graciously permitted the
leader to win with them. And I have yet to find any other
way of doing it.

In Stephen Crane's classic novel *The Red Badge of
Courage*, an incident he took from real life demonstrated
the power of personal rewards in controlling the efforts of
a group of people. While the new recruits in the green regiment were debating the "honorable" way of meeting the
Confederate attack—whether it would be cowardly to lie
down or to kneel instead of standing bravely in the face
of enemy fire—the old hands in the next regiment were
digging "like terriers after a rat." Although the afternoon
was humid and their officers were not yet on the scene to
order it, they were digging rifle pits and building earth-
works to crouch behind. They needed no greater motivation than the ominous rebel line on the horizon, which
was going to be much closer in a very short time. By the
time of the second Confederate attack, the new lads were
also dug in.

Unless you can afford the luxury of standing authori-
tatively over people who cannot escape, or of allowing
people to give you what cooperation they will, you need
to communicate the Basic Principle simply and authentically through your verbal and nonverbal messages. You
must demonstrate in word and deed, to the best of your
ability, that people who cooperate with you will receive
pleasure rather than pain, prestige rather than humiliation,
and purpose from their activities rather than a sense of
futility. They will share in the payoffs which make them
winners, as consistently as you can arrange it.

CHAPTER FIVE

Attitudes
and Expectations

Not only does each person who is winning or losing in life relate to other men and women according to his personality pattern, he also relates from a consistent set of attitudes and expectations. But while no one pattern is any more effective than any other in reaching one's goals, the attitudes and expectations people hold are critical to their success in dealing with others. They determine, to a major degree, how conscientiously one's methods and techniques are communicated and applied.

During the crucial, formative years of childhood, while he is developing his personality pattern, each youngster is also reaching a certain conclusion about his ability and worth. If a child is guided supportively toward maturity by competent and loving parents, he will most likely learn that he is a capable person who can do just about what he sets out to achieve, within broad physical and mental limits. Learning his worth allows a youngster to reach his junior or even senior high-school years before he makes his final decision about his place on life's totem pole. By that time he has developed a realistic understanding of his skills, interests, and abilities.

When a child is not given this luxury of time before

reaching a decision about his worth and ability, in a home where physical or psychological frustrations are great because the parents are indifferent, brutal, or simply ignorant, he makes decisions that have no relationship to reality. By the age of two or three, an emotionally deprived or physically abused child has developed an attitude about life or has learned such low expectations about himself that he is virtually a confirmed loser before he reaches kindergarten. This immature, anxious child forms a perceptual screen which later governs his achievements, earnings, sexual satisfaction, and even the length of his life before he can write his name. The most insidious thing he learns is that he is not free to act upon life, but must remain acted upon by forces, events, and people he cannot control. And few people ever go back to think through what they have interpreted as reality before they became adults, for they believe that what has happened to them is their fate.

A few such men and women are fortunate enough to learn that those disastrous childhood decisions, which were based on their frustrating experiences, can be changed, but the vast majority waste their lives without realizing they are living according to ideas they learned in infancy or early childhood. Youngsters who are under more pressure than they can handle set in motion negative, self-fulfilling, lifelong game plans and seldom have second thoughts about their truth.

Just as a Polynesian child cannot really understand why an Eskimo youngster needs eighteen different words to accurately describe the snow conditions upon which his survival depends, the losing child cannot understand that his attitudes and expectations are causing him to fail. So he goes through life blaming his parents, racial prejudice, society, or his teachers, no more realizing that he set the stage for himself as a child than the South Sea youngster can comprehend an Arctic winter. It is beyond his reality and he doesn't comprehend it. Without a breakthrough of some kind, he goes through life acting out a series of banal roles, living far below his potential, being acted upon by life rather than seizing it in his own grasp to make things happen the way he chooses. He is a perpetual loser.

Psychologists Viktor Frankl, Muriel James, and Thomas Harris report that each person has almost total control of the attitudes and expectations that determine whether he shall win or lose in life. Many people have read Norman Vincent Peale's *Power of Positive Thinking* or criticized Clement Stone's *Positive Mental Attitude* concepts without realizing that contemporary research has given scientific respectability to the idea that each person is living a game plan that was developed early in life. Once he realizes this, the plan can be revised to contain what he wants life to include, provided that he develops a vehicle with which to reach his goals.

The stage is set for becoming a winner or a loser by the dominant psychological attitudes each child accepts for himself according to the experiences he has. According to Harris, there are only four basic attitudes about life, love, and personal worth in relationships. These psychological attitudes can be called:

> The Superiority Attitude
> (I'm a winner and you're a loser.)
> The Inferiority Attitude
> (I'm a loser but you're a winner.)
> The Hopeless Attitude
> (We're both losers.)
> The Accepting Attitude
> (We're both winners.)

The Superiority Attitude
(I'm a winner but you're a loser.)

People who are not very observant sometimes call this a superiority complex, especially when the person using it is successful in carrying off his charade of self-worth. Actually it is a psychological overcompensation in which the user is protecting himself from consistently feeling like the loser he "learned" himself to be in an earlier stage of life. He was so badly crippled in dealing with other people that he cannot admit, especially to himself, that he is less than perfect. And since no one is perfect, his defenses soon become obvious to those who feel the sting of his criticism. They do not become visible to himself, however, for this would be painful and his perceptual screen keeps any distracting information from coming through.

This is one of the problems that contributed to Richard Nixon's downfall. In his relationships with the Congress, civil service workers, his staff, and the cabinet, he was never able to tolerate either advice or criticism. Even his closest assistants admitted that the meetings and discussions he held were only for show, since he arrived at them with his mind already made up, regardless of any new facts being presented.

Despite the way in which the man publicly idealized his parents, it's clear that something happened in Nixon's childhood home at Yorba Linda that froze him in such a position that he could never again admit to being wrong. When something unpleasant occurred, it had to be "their" fault; someone out there was to blame, since he could not be. A hard-ball Superiority player uses his perceptual screen to turn every failure around, to defend his shredded ego so that he can feel somewhat better about himself.

In Mr. Nixon's case, he would have destroyed the effectiveness of the F.B.I. and the C.I.A. and compromised the entire Justice Department to maintain his Superiority self-image. Finally, as he blamed the Eastern Liberal Establishment, the media, the Democratic party, the college students, the Indochinese, the Congress, and eventually his own Republican party for his troubles, the nation decided that it didn't want such a loser in the presidency and his support crumbled away. And, if his interviews with David Frost and the revelations of his memoirs are any indication, not one iota of blame has yet filtered through his perceptual screen.

This self-defensive attitude develops when a child who has been abused or ignored tries to make some sense out of his misery. He feels much better being alone than with the people who make him suffer. He begins to feel: "I can make it if they let me do things my way." Therefore he must be better than they, because they cause pain he does not feel when he is alone. Of course, he is too young to think in these terms, but the emotions are there: the world is a dangerous place and he is on his own for survival.

As an abused child, he sees no other option, since this attitude probably saves his sanity and his life. Yet when he acts out these perceptions in his interpersonal relationships, he becomes the classroom bully, the brutal drill instructor, the sadistic manager, the rogue cop, or the parent whose children become mentally ill. Certainly he is unable to convince people that he will share life's winnings with them, for no one really likes his condescension. He contributes to his own interpersonal failures, because he refuses to become introspective about the conflicts and rejections his psychological attitude triggers. All the unpleasant things his attitude causes are always someone else's fault.

Such a person is not always cruel or even selfish, at least to people who accept his dominance. He may treat his wife as "the little woman," a child whom he has to pamper. An engineer with this attitude may be very cooperative with the sales force, as if the men were a collection of idiots he has to pamper because they don't know a "turnbuckle from a drill motor." With this attitude he is often at the center of a conflict of some kind or another, as he sets straight all the idiots who clutter his life, causing the very problems he professes to detest.

The Inferiority Attitude
(I'm a loser but you're a winner.)

The next psychological attitude held by some people is the Inferiority one. This is the view held by people who respond to childhood abuse in a reversal of the Superiority attitude. Perhaps the pressure was greater or the child's innate resilience was less strong, so that he collapsed in surrender, accepting the "fact" that he or she was an inept person who was suited only to be led around by the winners in life. He has *learned* that he has some fatal flaw that cripples him as he tries to cope with life and others.

From time to time, such a person wins a round in life and feels good about it for a while, though he usually sees his win as a stroke of luck from a kindly Providence rather than the result of his ability. He spends a lot of time waiting for his luck to change or for the winners who consistently beat him to toss him their leavings. A person learns this psychological attitude when, as a child, he sees that the adults around him are so much more competent than he that he gives up competing. He fails to see that their superiority is only a result of age and maturity as his godlike parents teach him that he is incompetent.

Edith Bunker of *All in the Family* lives with this attitude as she waits for Archie and everyone else to tell her what to do, since she feels too incompetent to make important decisions for herself. Unfortunately, some people like Edith try to find a Superiority player to relieve their anxieties by taking charge of their lives. On the surface, this would seem like a fine arrangement, since it meets both their needs. The fact is that it seldom works out. The "winner" in the relationship resents having to carry the "loser" along by himself, while the "loser" resents, however unconscious his anger, playing second fiddle to someone who acts out his part more successfully.

At one of the colleges where I taught, there were two young professors who held Superiority attitudes because of their degrees, publications, and academic achievements. It was silly, since we all had comparable degrees, numerous published articles, and prestige, but these things served to hide their insecurities. Interestingly enough, both of them had married men with Inferiority attitudes and both marriages failed. Since they were in my division, I had an opportunity to observe them professionally and socially for several years as their marriages were collapsing.

Beth was a smiling Supporter, like myself, so we initially got along better than Anna and I did. And while Beth would avoid criticism until her stress caused her to attack her husband, Anna the Entertainer would attack him as soon as tension occurred and then acquiesce with a simmering anger that kept her in tension. Nevertheless, the message both sent to their husbands and peers was that they were inferior. The two young men seemed to accept it as their just rewards for being so inept, but both women eventually left them anyway.

Even when an Inferiority player is successful, he rarely enjoys the fruits of his labors and has to plunge harder and harder into more work to prove to himself that he is actually better than the way he sees himself. He can rarely relax and enjoy his reward.

The Hopeless Attitude
(We're both losers.)

The third attitude is one that is doubly cursed, that people are all impotent fools who are doomed to suffer and lose as hopeless victims of fate all through life. The frustrations such a person felt in childhood when his psychological attitude was developing were so severe that he rejected both his own worth and that of his parents. In adulthood, his attitude usually drives away anyone who feels either superior or inferior for he is a disciple of despair.

Not only were such inept, frustrated people like assassins Lee Harvey Oswald and Sirhan Sirhan hopeless losers, as they lashed out to kill the Kennedy brothers, so were philosophical writers like Camus and Sartre, who were disciples of hopelessness, though they attacked society with words rather than with guns. I suspect that they cause infinitely more harm than the physically violent among the Hopeless, however. In any case, their verbal and nonverbal communication reveals their attitudes to those around them and they have lost the interpersonal contest for commitment before they ever learn that they can become winners by changing life to meet their needs.

The Accepting Attitude
(We're both winners.)

A person's psychological attitude may be hidden from casual observers, but it plays a major role in one's winning or losing with others, since it is eventually revealed, through nonverbal communication, to the people who remain close. The first three attitudes are the deep-seated negative beliefs about life and achievement that losers hold. Not one of the three can help a person become a consistent winner, though someone like Howard Hughes may earn millions of dollars through his companies. For though he earned a fortune with his mental ability, he remained a loser in virtually every other aspect of his life, eventually starving himself to death in despair. Only the Accepting attitude that we are both winners can produce the respect, commitment, and love needed to make life successful.

The Accepting attitude means that the holder can accept who he is, despite his recognition of the inevitable human flaws all people have, share the rewards and prestige with those he relates to positively, and accept them as worthwhile men and women whose feelings, goals, and achievements are as important to them as his feelings are to himself. Because he feels this way about himself and others, he doesn't go out of his way to win status by hurting them, by devaluing them, or by cheating them of their payoffs. He is going to be frustrated and angry at times, as all people are, and he handles these emotions according to his personality pattern. But he doesn't manufacture an illogical view of his worth and ability to meet deep-seated psychological fears. He is secure enough to apologize when he is wrong, to express love or affection when he feels it, and to fight for what he believes is right, all the while accepting the fact that people are pretty much all right when they are treated decently.

The Accepting attitude, which must be harnessed to a productive life-style in order to produce a consistent winner, is more than a temporary feeling of goodwill. It is the healthy position that enables a person to relate effectively and well with a wide variety of men and women, a powerful philosophy of achievement and positive human relationships. Having this attitude doesn't mean that you will be universally successful, of course. Few people have ever been more accepting than Abraham Lincoln, and he failed at virtually everything he ever attempted in his first fifty years of life. But when his big chance came, he did more to hold the Union together than any other person or combination of persons. He did it by gathering together a cabinet of powerful, temperamental men, many of whom ridiculed his frontier mannerisms and anecdotes from their Superiority attitudes. He tolerated them because he knew who he was and what he was worth. His ultimate payoff on the spiritual level made it all worthwhile.

Lincoln had his fears and doubts. Not to have them would have been impossible for such self-centered, striving creatures as people are. But since he built on the bedrock of a good psychological attitude which enabled him to work effectively, hold high expectations, and not care too much who got the credit, he was instrumental in saving the Union. You have only to compare his effectiveness with that of his counterpart, Jefferson Davis, who tried to deal with such powerful men as Jackson and Lee from his defensive Superiority attitude. There was much more to winning or losing the Civil War than the attitudes of the opposing presidents, but they played a consequential part in the results, nevertheless.

People who want to become consistent winners must learn enough about human motivation, their own needs, and life to be self-assured as they plan independently for themselves, while cooperating and competing appropriately under different circumstances. They must accept that people come from a wide variety of family backgrounds, which filter down to four basic personality patterns and four psychological attitudes. They find rewards that are effective as they relate supportively according to their knowledge. Most importantly, they realize that one cannot demand dedication and commitment any longer, so they learn how to negotiate the rewards of relationships with enough people so that their own payoffs are the ones they want from life.

To the personality pattern chart I have added the psychological attitudes one can hold. The outer ring can be rotated mentally, to set the attitude held by a person over his own personality pattern. Doing that will give you a much better view of how he or she will respond to you.

An Accepting person will give you the respect, cooperation, support, and appropriate competition you deserve. He expects and will respond positively to the same things from you. If you hold an Accepting attitude, you can consistently win cooperation from others as they follow the Law of Reciprocity that you use.

From a Superiority person you can expect criticism, de-

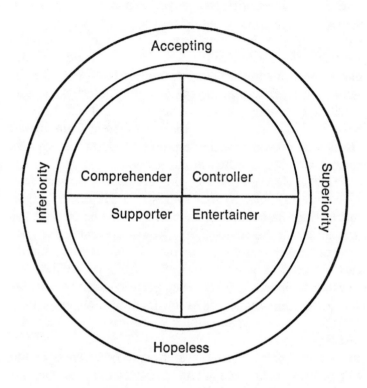

valuation, inappropriate competition, and disagreement. He wants you to yield to his demands, but will despise you if you do, unless you show that you are as strong as he wants to be. If you are dealing with others from a Superiority attitude, you are causing most of your interpersonal problems as people hook into your scorn and anger, also according to the Law of Reciprocity. Back away from pointless conflicts as much as possible, since they only let you win some battles while losing the war for commitment. Don't despise the people who cannot disguise their feelings of inadequacy as well as you, since most people will read your nonverbal communication well enough to avoid you as much as possible.

From an Inferiority person you can expect envy, fear, demands for help, and subtle resistance. He wants you to simplify his life, but resents any attempts to do so, for it only confirms his inadequacies. If you are living with this burden from childhood, stop to realize that you have the same hours per day as anyone else, the libraries and universities are there for you to improve yourself, and you have a mind that is not a whole lot different from anyone else's. You must accept the responsibility for your own life, since it cannot be shifted to anyone else.

From a Hopeless person you can expect despair, fear, rage, and resistance to your suggestions. He doesn't expect much, since he believes you are as inept as he feels. If you are successful in some activity, he will attribute it to good luck or to dishonesty on your part. If this is your attitude, realize that it is a total fabrication from your childhood, in which an immature, frightened person made the decisions that have limited your achievements until the present time. Start using new ways to win for yourself in life, rather than insisting that no one can win. Plenty of people are winning in love, business, education, and many other areas of life, but none of them do until they understand that they are responsible for most of what they come home with.

The Power of Expectations

Researchers and therapists are just now beginning to understand the dramatic power that faith, imagination, and expectations hold over each person's life. The men and women who have been hurt so badly in childhood that they live with one of the three losing attitudes feel like victims of fate. But that doesn't nullify what has been discovered by medical and psychological researchers during the past twenty years. It is not a cliché, as so many losers believe, but a fact as consistent as the force of gravity, that attitudes and expectations determine whether we lose or win in life's contests. As a result of our childhood experiences, each person reaches adulthood with a self-fulfilling game plan, which determines what happens to him throughout life. He has a set of expectations which either defy failure, illness, and premature death, or which program them into his life.

Researchers Simonton and Klopfer have found evidence that they feel shows that attitudes and expectations not only determine how well we live, but what each person eventually dies of. Simonton was Chief of Radiology for the U.S. Air Force and is now a prominent tumor specialist in Dallas. Klopfer is a leading psychodiagnostician and author from U.C.L.A., a man whose books I have used for my own work and required of my students for decades.

They report that they have discovered a direct link associating human personality patterns, attitudes, and expectations with malignant tumors. The two men wrote that a positive set of values and an accepting attitude about life increases the odds against developing cancer. Simonton said that a positive life-style, lived with high expectations, sends silent thunderbolts of resistance to keep malignant cells under control. Klopfer, however, went beyond that to develop a paper-and-pencil test which identified, he reported, the men and women who were going to develop malignant tumors in the future. Obviously, a test like that cannot measure physical differences such as blood count, chemical states, and so on, but can only deal with intangible attitudes and expectations. Yet the test is reported to be very accurate. To summarize, the researchers have discovered that a person who feels good about life and himself, who lives with a positive attitude, and who holds high expectations as he becomes deeply involved in things that are important to him, lives longer and more successfully than a person who does not.

For centuries scholars have known that men and women who were doing a responsible task from a positive attitude had a better chance of surviving than those who did not.

For example, doctors and nurses have long been observed to work for months in the midst of epidemics that were killing thousands of people, without contracting the disease they were combating. Perceptive writers have wondered about this obvious ability in the days before vaccines were developed. The bodily defenses were isolated both by Carl Hoff of Austria and by myself when I was psychology chairman at Westminster College.

I took ten psychology majors—alert, healthy young men and women—all of whom were good hypnotic subjects, as I had discovered in previous experiments. I placed the ten in deep hypnotic trances and left them with the post-hypnotic suggestion that they were all working at tasks they felt were important to themselves and to society, happy in their relationships, and deeply satisfied with life. Then they were awakened, given time for their bio-chemistry to stabilize, and blood samples were taken. The blood was then analyzed by a university laboratory. The same procedure was followed a week later, but with one major difference. In the second hypnotic session the youngsters were left with the suggestion that life was deeply dissatisfying for them, they were in interpersonal conflict, and their work was unimportant. Blood samples were drawn and analyzed once more.

The results were astonishing, to say the least. I found that for each student, without exception, the agglutination titer against bacilli infection was many times higher when the students felt a deep satisfaction with life. There was not a single exception to this, thus demonstrating why a doctor or nurse who feels good about his work and himself when working in an epidemic has much more effective physical defenses against disease. The values, attitudes, and expectations you hold about life, others, and yourselves often mean survival in life-or-death situations. They always mean the difference between losing or winning in your everyday activities.

Expecting to Win

Children who develop the winning attitude from their early years, who are taught that they can control life instead of remaining helpless pawns of fate, start taking charge of the events that make people losers or winners at an early age. They master the techniques that shape life by learning from their parents. If you were not fortunate enough in your selection of parents and grandparents, don't assume that you cannot change, for that is what *Nice Guys Finish First* is all about: changing the attitudes and concepts that hamper you.

Men and women who understand the power of expectations usually rear their children to expect a great deal from life and from themselves. Families like the Kennedys, Rockefellers, and Mellons convince their children they will grow up to be governors, senators, and presidents, manage multinational corporations, and shape science and the arts with their power. And, most often, they do! If one of the parents has emotional problems that might hamper the growth of a child, the family hires competent nurses, nannies, and tutors to see that the youngsters learn to hold high expectations. They are sent to excellent private schools and Ivy League colleges to sharpen their minds, expand their contacts, and develop their skills to a high degree. Few things are left to chance.

This process takes place so regularly that one businessman jokingly said that he hates hiring Harvard or Yale graduates for jobs in his company. He laughed as he explained that they all expect to start work as vice-presidents —but I noticed, however, that he hired them. They have the kind of expectations that a manager wants his young employees to hold!

In less prosperous families, boys and girls with just as much innate ability and intelligence are taught that they will grow up to be carpenters, policemen, hairdressers, and secretaries. And they usually grow up planning to become what they believe they can be.

Expecting to become a winner isn't the result of having family power or money so much as having the imagination and intelligence to recognize one's ability to change life for the better. Edsel Ford was reared in conflict between an Inferiority-feeling mother and a Superiority father who was unable to tolerate any deviation from his iron-fisted rule of the family as well as the company, while the mother spent her time darning socks and attending séances, until Edsel felt like he could not win. Therefore he never did make the effort.

Josephine Churchill lived a banal, losing life-style despite all the power and prestige her father Winston had at his command. She never caught sight of what she could become, and life was a continual disappointment for her.

While no one can deny the advantages a wealthy family can give children, a lack of wealth or power isn't as great a handicap as many people believe. Being born poor simply forces a person to function in a different manner if he plans on becoming a winner. Jeno Paulucci was a poor son of immigrant parents who grew up on the Iron Range of Minnesota. But he realized that life was his to shape, so he borrowed a few hundred dollars to form the Chun-King Chinese food company. He sold ChunKing some years later for many millions of dollars.

In contrast, Edwin Edwards grew up on a small farm near my father's place in Louisiana. He seemed no different from the other boys and girls in my class in school, but somehow his parents made the entire family feel like people are the masters of their fate. As this is written, my old childhood chum has been a congressman for years and has served as governor of Louisiana for several terms, despite his humble beginnings.

Each person can be said to have a positive or a negative electrode to his life, according to Berne. A negative electrode draws failure and disappointment like an old-fashioned lightning rod attracts electricity from the sky. A negative electrode draws failure and unhappiness, because they are compatible with one's expectations. It brings destructive friends, self-devaluation, unplanned pregnancies, ill health, and early death. A man or a woman with a negative electrode feels that he is jinxed by bad luck, when he is actually bringing most of it on himself by his lifestyle. It is part of his self-fulfilling game plan, which was formed when he was a confused, two- or three-year-old child.

On the other hand, a positive electrode attracts good preparation, thoughtful decisions, supportive friends, and bold ventures. And the winning events that result from this kind of game plan are no more the result of luck than is a losing life. Winning events, when they occur, have been carefully planned for and are fully expected.

I don't want to give the impression that winning or losing in life is connected to the amount of money you earn, for that is not the case. Certainly a ghetto youngster who fights to earn an education in Chicago and Detroit and invests her life lovingly teaching children is a real winner in every aspect of the word. So is the farm boy who enjoys working the land and rears his children with positive attitudes and high expectations as he makes a living for them from a modest farm in Colorado or Kansas. The crucial aspect is the realization that you can shape life as you want it to become, rather than being acted upon by forces and people beyond your control.

What expectations do you have about your ability to mold life to suit yourself? Did you "learn" that you have to narcotize yourself before you can enjoy making love, that people from your family are weak and sickly, that life is supposed to be short and grim rather than long and happy? Many parents teach their children such things and worse, and wonder why the youngsters never mature beyond their expectations.

The mother of Eric Hoffer, the longshoreman-philosopher, actually taught him that he would never live more than forty years because the Hoffers were short-lived. Fortunately for the human race, he didn't believe it, for all of his books were written in the second forty years of his life. On the other hand, Eric Berne, the father of Transactional Analysis, did believe that the Bernes lived an austere, unloving life that characteristically did not last very long.

In his book, *What Do You Say After You Say Hello?* Berne considered, in much detail, the negative game plans many people unthinkingly live by. He called them "scripts" and stated that they damage lives more than we realize. In the book, which was his last, he wrote extensively about the many men and women he had known who programmed coronaries for themselves without realizing what they were doing. And Berne, with his strong Comprehending personality pattern, achieved greatly but failed to consistently live warmly and accepting of others. As a result he probably programmed his own death. He did have his fatal heart attack at the same age, to the day, as his mother's coronary. He lingered on for a week or so, but he died as he expected to die, following a "script" of his own making.

The childhood experiences which you have based your life upon are irredeemably in the past, so they cannot be changed now. You do have the ability to change your attitudes and to improve your expectations, however, to the day you die. You can learn whatever skills and knowledge you need to develop the plan or vehicle which will make you a constant winner. You simply cannot *expect* to win, waiting for some Superiority player to win for you. To become a winner, you have to invest the time you have available and the skills you can develop.

CHAPTER SIX

Applying Praise
Effectively

From the explanations and descriptions of the concepts I've discussed in the preceding chapters, you may have assumed that I would recommend a lavish use of praise in almost every situation. That is not correct, for using praise to reward behavior can be compared to using a powerful medicine. When it is applied carefully for specific reasons, it works miracles. If it is used indiscriminately and too frequently, it either loses its effectiveness or becomes dangerous.

One of the worst offenders I ever knew used a continuous litany of meaningless praise as he moved through his department, patting people on the back and slapping rumps until all his workers sincerely hoped he'd choke on his artificial good humor. He had an Entertaining pattern, but had never learned to use it effectively, so his praise did more harm than good as his workers rejected it as a means to manipulate them to do things that rewarded him but not themselves.

In a recent business seminar a manager expressed the confusion people sometimes experience when they attempt to use praise indiscriminately when helping others work with them. Fred said:

> We had some labor trouble in our company. It hadn't yet reached a point where a strike was inevitable, but the workers and managers were in an adversary relationship. There was some sabotage and a large increase in scrap, waste, and absenteeism. One section held steady all the way, however. The men kept scrap to a minimum, came to work regularly, and kept their production at a normal level.
>
> I thought about it for a long time before I decided that they deserved some recognition. So, one day during the lunch hour, I stopped to tell them how much I appreciated their work. I told them that I was proud of their loyalty and would remember it. My speech was a total disaster! Not one of the men said a word; so, after a long, embarrassed silence, I left. Within two days their production was down and the men had started calling in sick.
>
> What really angered me was how they repaid me for going out of my way to recognize their work. I always thought praise was a good way to have people continue doing good things. What went wrong?

A few days later I took the time to find out why his praise backfired. I met several of the workers when they agreed to talk to me at a café after the shift was over. They told me their version of the episode. It was as I expected. Among themselves, the men had quietly agreed that they were not going to penalize their section supervisor by calling in sick or by lowering production and quality. They respected him too much for that, though they had wondered among themselves what the other employees thought about them for not cooperating in the slowdown. The section workers *all* felt guilty about supporting the supervisor rather than the rest of the workers. The manager's praise, at precisely the wrong time and for the wrong reasons, brought the matter to a head and they could no longer straddle the fence. His praise brought everything into focus; their guilt feelings solidified, and they found relief in the only way open to them in a company where an adversary relationship existed.

The Fine Art of Praise

A common misconception that psychologically inexperienced people make is that because some praise is good, more praise is better. As Fred discovered, this is not necessarily true. Praise which is undeserved or given at the wrong time can cause resentment and destroy commitment. It has to be used as a payoff and it has to be connected to good things happening, as I discussed in the first chapter on motivation. When you tell someone that he's been a great help and that you expect more from him in the future, he has been singled out from his peers. He may have trouble accepting the praise and future expectations for any number of reasons.

His self-image may not be compatible with the one you hold. In addition, you may be forcing him to a higher level of commitment than he is ready to make. He may also know that he doesn't deserve the praise, and may thus develop guilt feelings. A worker may have recently foisted a box of marginal parts on a careless inspector. Perhaps a student has decided to drop your class because the way you grade or teach displeases him. A child may have been planning how he can get even with an older brother or sister, or perhaps fantasizing that the sibling had been kidnapped by terrorists.

When a person has ambivalent feelings about himself, a confused self-image, or resentment toward you, the unwarranted praise he receives will only confuse him. He may resent it and feel he has to reveal his "true" character. Often the contrary reactions he has when receiving praise is his unconscious way of trying to remain true to his own self-concepts and image.

You can take a number of simple precautions to help

you use praise as a reward for behavior you want repeated. Praise should be reserved for those times when it is needed or deserved. You should focus on work and achievement rather than on appearance, personality, or character. Commendations must be deserved, you must be authentic, and the timing should be correct. Here is an example of how praise can focus on performance rather than on character.

Marge, a scriptwriter for a television studio, had taken a difficult assignment and completed it ahead of schedule in an excellent manner. She had been assigned only to write the script, but she researched it first, put it into an interesting form, and, when the producer was injured, stepped in to do the production planning and work as well. Her manager, Jerry, was pleased and talked to the young woman about her contributions to the group. Jerry said:

> *Jerry*: That was a monstrous job to do, especially with Bob out like he was. I didn't believe it could be done in five weeks.
>
> *Marge*: I had my doubts, too. Having to substitute for Bob and everything.
>
> *Jerry*: It was a superb job of researching, writing, and producing.
>
> *Marge*: It was the hardest thing I've ever done.
>
> *Jerry*: Well, it didn't show. The whole project was so professional! It's a pleasure to have a job turn out so nice.
>
> *Marge*: I really enjoyed doing it.
>
> *Jerry*: Thanks so much.
>
> *Marge*: Thank you for having such faith in me.

Jerry's well-chosen words of praise were matched to the accomplishment. They focused on what Marge had done, not on her character. It was effective praise, and the psychological payoff guaranteed that she would do her best the next time she had a project to do for him.

On the other hand, the following statements of praise, which focus on a person's character or personality, are not as useful as they first seem, because they are too intense.

> What would I *ever* do around here without you?
> You're a wonderful person to help so much.
> You're the greatest writer in the world!
> No one else could have done what you did.

Such comments frequently disturb and threaten people for several reasons. At the very least they leave the recipient with the nagging doubt that you are not telling the truth. This is especially true if you use praise too frequently and glibly. It also leaves many people wondering what to do for an encore; they wonder what you will think about them if they are unable to live up to your grand, sweeping statements. Instead of waiting to be pushed into a situation where their feared shortcomings are exposed to view, they unconsciously set the speaker straight about their "real" capabilities by failing in some way.

When praise is too direct, it fails to have the effect you want. A large number of people have trouble handling praise openly if they are told that they are *great and wonderful* human beings. It is difficult for people to openly accept statements that they are brilliant and superior without occasionally worrying what will happen to the relationship when they blunder. Make it easy for the person you are praising to accept psychological or spiritual rewards for an accomplishment without pushing him to a total commitment or to a level he cannot feel comfortable on all the time.

Statements and Inferences

It is usually more effective to infer praise, so the listener can discern positive things about himself and the relationship without becoming anxious or pushed from his comfort zone. It can be done like this: Jessie, an editorial assistant, had come in on Saturday morning to proof and correct an article needed for her magazine's Monday morning deadline. As she worked, she discovered a serious error that the author and the researcher had both missed. Obviously, her editor was pleased. He said:

> *Editor*:   That was an obscure thing to catch. It must have
> been hard to spot.
> *Jessie*:   I seem to notice inconsistencies like that.
> *Editor*:   You're showing real talent for the publishing busi-
> ness.
> *Jessie*:   Hey! Maybe I won't stay an assistant forever.
> *Editor*:   I wouldn't be surprised!

Notice how the editor talked about the difficulty of finding the error. He let Jessie make the cognitive transfer about her ability. Simply telling her that she was a "bright girl" or telling her that she was "wonderful" would have had less of an impact than the way it was handled.

Effective praise has two basic components in giving payoffs. First, the verbal and nonverbal messages must remain consistent, or you will appear insincere. Second, you should be aware of the recipient's emotional response and nonverbal feedback and be ready to modify your praise to fit his need. Praise can be like a blank chalkboard upon which an outline is sketched so the receiver can fill in the blanks with the positive reinforcement he can accept. Here are some examples that people have suggested in seminars I have conducted for parents, teachers, and managers.

> *Productive Praise*   Thanks for cleaning the kitchen. Your
> effort made it look nice again.
> *Possible Reaction*   That was a nice thing for me to do. Mom
> really appreciates my help.
> *Ineffective Praise*   You're really a doll to help me.
> *Productive Praise*   The suggestion you had about data pro-
> cessing impressed the boss. It was complete, but to the
> point. He'll use it right away.
> *Possible Reaction*   My ideas are worth something around
> here. I'll keep my eyes open in the future.

Ineffective Praise   That was pure genius. You're always in
   front of the crew.

Productive Praise   Your talk to the PTA about teacher cut-
   backs stirred a lot of interest in our financial problems.

Possible Reaction   I'm glad I did my homework well. When
   I work at it I can communicate so others really understand me.

Ineffective Praise   You're a great public speaker for someone so young.

Productive Praise   The facts you researched got my program
   through the church board last night. We'll get the budget
   we need.

Possible Reaction   That was well worth the time I spent on it.
   He really uses my work.

Ineffective Praise   What would I ever do without you?

Productive praise and the recipient's logical conclusions
about your perception of him can form a lasting bond and
provide mutual rewards. Since people consistently move
to meet positive expectations held by people they trust and
respect, such statements can be used to shape performance
without causing fear of disappointment or resentment. They
are truthful, appropriate, and deserved—and both of you
know it. They do not demand a total commitment the recipient is not ready to make, though that door has been
left open. He knows, should he make a mistake in the
future, that you will not throw him to the wolves. He can
be authentic and honest with you and perhaps set his sights
a little higher next time.

The Art of Criticism

Anyone in a leadership role of any kind, whether in the
home, classroom, or business office, realizes that there are
times when he has to demand better performance, punish
someone who has refused to cooperate, or set some issue
straight. Regardless of your good intentions at such a time,
correction and criticism is not pleasant to the person re-

ceiving your attention. You can, however, improve your skills at correcting people so that it does not cost you good-will and cooperation.

It rarely does any good to deal with motives, character, or might-have-beens when someone has failed or blundered. Unfortunately, at times of crisis, many people are more interested in maintaining their comfort or fixing blame than they are in resolving problems.

David, a divisional chairman in a state university, had sought and received funding to develop a new research program when two of the key professors unexpectedly resigned to accept positions in another university. David's schedule was ruined and he was called in to report to the academic vice-president of the school. The administrator exploded in frustration and anger.

> *Dean*:   I've told you before not to put all your eggs in one basket! You should have planned around such a possibility before it happened.
>
> *David*:   Those two never leaked a word about their intentions to leave. There was nothing in the wind about another offer.
>
> *Dean*:   It looks to me like you don't have the foresight needed to manage the work of your division.
>
> *David*:   No one could have foreseen their leaving!
>
> *Dean*:   The right man in the job would have made some contingency plans or seen through their intentions. Can't you ever be relied on?
>
> *David*:   Listen! You may think you have the right to talk to me this way, but you haven't. You get off my back or I'll take this to the Association. And the members will back me up!

Productive criticism or correction, which leads to winning relationships, deals with only the important issues and how to correct mistakes. Character flaws, motivation, and commitment must be considered only when the atmosphere is calm and when authentic praise can be used to counteract the unpleasantness the criticism is sure to produce.

Even at that time, however, you can use terms and concepts that are supportive and lead to higher expectations for the future.

When Larry, a salesman for a small printing firm, wrecked his company automobile on an icy bridge, the owner reacted calmly. He said:

> It was insured, so don't worry about it. Here are the keys to my car. I'll use my family sedan until we can get a new one. When you get over the shock, get out in the territory. Our customers will be expecting you.

The salesman, who had recently left an adversary relationship in his previous company, sighed deeply in relief and could hardly believe that the boss was through with the matter. All he could do was stammer his thanks and return to work with a determination to do his best for the man he worked for.

The owner did not lecture Larry on how he could have saved the car had he been driving more cautiously. Neither did he offer a lecture on the costs of insurance coverage for the firm. Nothing he could have said would have restored the car, and none of his advice would have taught Larry anything the accident hadn't. Later the manager told me about his feelings. He said:

> I was tempted to let him have it, I admit. But I remembered your seminar and realized that my frustrations were high and it was my relief I was largely concerned with. When I backed down the poor boy almost cried in relief. But I did play a ferocious game of racquet ball that afternoon to end my tension. Larry has become a top producer for me, and our good relationship goes back to my not gaining relief at his expense that day.

The High Cost of Insults

Few managers, teachers, pastors, or parents have the power to insult people or to express their anger without paying a terrible price. Not only do they end up as losers: because they cannot gain commitment, they keep everyone else from winning. And in the case of parents, they may actually be destroying any chance the youngsters have of learning how to live effectively. In most cases conflicts result from men and women feeling frustrated because of the pressures of life. Rarely are the nagging little squabbles that complicate the harnessing of a group's talents and skills caused by deep philosophical issues. Most of the time managers and other leaders insult people because they have been forced from their comfort zones by circumstances. Then few people care whether anything good or supportive happens, since they are simply going along because of their own reasons. They have become adversaries and commitment is not very likely to occur.

Janet, a bookkeeper in an insurance office, was unable to balance the books Dennis, her manager, needed for his monthly report to the home office. Anxious, because he feared that sales were still below quota for the month, Dennis stormed into Janet's office, leaned over her, and demanded:

> *Dennis*: Come on! Come on! How many times are you going to go through that thing before you find your mistake?
>
> *Janet*: There's a simple mistake somewhere. I just don't see it yet.
>
> *Dennis*: Simple mistake, hell. It's one of your classier goofs, and you know it. You could do better than this if you'd care about your work!
>
> *Janet*: You should talk! If you had gotten the reports to me on time, I wouldn't be rushing so frantically.
>
> *Dennis*: That's enough of your talk! Your job here is to do what I want, when I want it. Nothing else!
>
> *Janet*: I wait for days, while you play golf with the salesmen, and then I have to listen to this. No wonder we're behind quota!
>
> *Dennis*: One more word out of you and you'll be out looking for another job.

Janet: Is that a promise?
Dennis: You had better believe it!

At that point the young woman stood, closed her books, carried them to the wastebasket, and threw them in.

Janet: Your new *girl* can probably find the problem in a week or two. Have a *nice* weekend, Dennis!

She got her purse and a few belongings from her desk and walked away, leaving Dennis suddenly wondering how he was going to placate the Hartford office once more when his reports were late.

Men and women are not robots, and their minds do not operate like computers. There is an ebb and flow to human attitudes and emotions. You must plan to correct people when both you and the other person are in your comfort zone, and make the corrections without insults if you want them to be accepted. Most people will accept a noninsulting correction as a learning experience.

I have always suspected that there is one major reason why people often do such a poor job in using correction techniques. It seems to me, though I cannot verify it with research, that the primary motivation in most criticism is to prove to one's self that he or she is not to blame. If the tail can be pinned on the donkey (Janet, in the anecdote above), people like Dennis can assure themselves that they are not at fault. They have found a scapegoat for their feelings of inadequacy and their perceptual screens keep out any facts that would contradict their assumptions. It seems not to matter that the mistake could be corrected supportively; the person is intent on punishing the blunderer loudly and often publicly.

Anger and Effectiveness

Few people learn to handle anger well, yet it is a fact of life and leadership. No doubt an angry response to frustration goes back to man's prehistoric experiences when he was struggling to survive on the savannah of Africa. For eons he feared the dangers on every hand, but he could only flee from them or outwit his enemies. No wonder the race became so self-centered that it verges on paranoia. Of course, it is not really paranoia when the wolves and big cats are lurking outside the cave every night, waiting for the fire to die down so they can dine—on you!

Parents still teach their children that experiencing anger is evil. Worse, people feel a curious mixture of relief and guilt when they act out their hostilities and frustrations. The relief acts as a payoff for expressing their anger verbally or nonverbally, while the guilt acts as a retardant. Sometimes, however, the pressures mount so high that they must be acted upon.

People often start the day in a good mood and with high expectations, but run into a traffic tie-up on the freeway, feel stress at being late for a crucial meeting, feel resentment from the people for whom their tardiness has created tension, and have an unsatisfying conclusion to the session. Bit by bit, in a typical day, their capacity to absorb any more tension is used up, until their "basket" is filled. Then no more can be accepted until the basket is emptied. And the basket-dumping process can be done with sophistication or with very little class. In his basket-emptying, Dennis used no sophistication at all with Janet, and she refused to accept it.

When a person has been pushed out of his comfort zone, he may experience what is almost a temporary form of insanity. He says and does things that not only are irrational, he doesn't even mean them. He becomes paranoid about the motives of others, insults them, threatens them, or withdraws inappropriately, depending on his personality pattern and his ability to tolerate frustration. When the episode is over and he feels better because his basket is empty once more, he feels a sense of relief, but also guilt, as he vows never to repeat his unfortunate performance. But unless he deliberately learns ways to control conflict while keeping his tension and stress at an acceptable level, the pressures of life will frustrate him sooner or later and he will have another episode. Either that, or he will destroy the plumbing that keeps him alive. Control of conflict will be the subject of an entire chapter later in *Nice Guys Finish First*.

Anger is as universal as any other emotion, and the pretense that it is not only makes one much more vulnerable to its effects. For, while an Entertainer will attack frustration-producing people and situations at once and a Supporter will do the same later, men and women from all four patterns do feel largely the same reaction to frustration and danger.

Anger is too strong an emotion to spend foolishly on small gains. When it is used, it must be valid, authentic, appropriate, and controlled. First, it should help you gain the relief to do your job better, or at least keep you from failing to reach your goals. Second, it should help people gain a better understanding of your limits. It will confuse people more if you attempt never to show anger than if you become frustrated and act out once in a while. Of course, it should go without saying that your anger should be expressed in such a way that you do not alienate the people around you. Assaulting people doesn't end anger, but merely passes it around the group from one person to another until it comes back to haunt you in a new form. To express your frustration you can say:

> When I plan an outing for the family and no one tells me that they are not coming, I become furious. I feel like my work is being devalued.
>
> It makes me unhappy when all the departments do not reach their goals. I wonder what I've done wrong.

When I fight New York for raises and then productivity falls, I wonder why I stuck my neck out. I feel like never putting my reputation on the line for anyone again.

When the whole family waits for the car on a night when we're going to the movies and you keep it with Mary Ann, I become furious. I feel like never loaning it to you again.

It never helps to vent one's anger on anyone in front of his peers. He may think of his family and financial needs and keep his mouth shut to keep his job or privileges, but he has rejected your intelligence and judgment. He will see few reasons why he should give you any commitment. He is usually determined to maintain his self-respect in some way rather than seeming a nonentity who can be abused without fear of retaliation. To create emotional shock waves that rebound through any group is to limit commitment and productivity. And that makes you the loser!

In dealing with your anger or the anger of others, remember that people are rarely consistent emotionally. People all have peaks and valleys as their feelings ebb and flow. People will become frustrated and thus will frustrate you in turn if nothing is being accomplished. At times, however, you will be the villain who makes people angry. But as long as the trade-offs balance over the months, men and women will accept the fact that you are human rather than a computerized robot. Don't try to hide your dissatisfaction or anger, but learn how to express it supportively. In the first place, you cannot hide it except at a great cost to yourself, for your nonverbal communication will give you away.

Men and women or boys and girls will become frustrated and angry with each other at times despite your best efforts to keep things going smoothly. Few of them will have the insights into human attitudes and behavior that you will have after reading *Nice Guys Finish First*. Use the information and methods here to prepare for times of frustration, and nip them in the bud with acceptance and support.

By being authentic in expressing your anger without insults or confrontations, you keep your own basket from filling and end resentment without doing things that simply pass it around in the group as first one person and then another finds a convenient empty basket into which to dump his frustrations. Expressing anger supportively depends on your being authentic enough to realize what you are feeling in time to do something before stress sets in and you act immaturely.

PART TWO

Negotiating
the Payoffs
(Identifying Needs and Problems)

CHAPTER SEVEN

Creating
Interpersonal Awareness

To consistently win the commitment of the men and women
you want to influence, you must get into their worlds by
accepting personality patterns, deemphasizing your own
ego needs, and offering rewards that are contingent upon
their cooperating with you. The people with whom you
want to share the winnings must be met on their own terms,
for they will help you gain what you want from life only
when you help them meet their needs and keep their trust.
After all, there are so many manipulators and confidence
artists who never share winnings that most people are right-
fully cautious about an unproven relationship.

You should also realize, when persuading people to do
what you want, that you don't have to be a supersalesman,
a tough labor arbitrator, or a psychotherapist to be effective. Not long ago I was conducting a seminar for educa-
tional tutors in a Southern city when one of the volunteers
asked a question that was important to her. Irene said:

> I'm up in the upper left sector of your personality-pattern
> chart, so I'm a Comprehender. I'm really shy about revealing
> my needs and feelings. Does this mean that I'll not be able to
> negotiate the way I want to?

What Irene was asking, I decided as I listened to her, was whether one's personality pattern had to be in any particular area for a person to become effective in winning commitment. No doubt a Controller could ask the same question, since he is not usually as willing to ask people what they want in a relationship. He tends to be more directive in his approach to interpersonal relationships. Of course I answered Irene with an emphatic "No!" If I believed otherwise I would not have written this book.

If you look at negotiation as an attempt to trick other people into giving away something for nothing—an effort to overwhelm them with words, logic, or demands, as an Entertainer sometimes does when forced from his comfort zone—you could assume that undemonstrative people who dislike competition might be at a disadvantage. This isn't persuasion, however, but the use of personal power to command compliance with a predetermined plan which may or may not be rewarding to anyone else.

Persuading or negotiating, as taught here, is not as complex as enticing others to let you have all the payoffs. It is simply sharing the rewards of life—whether in the home, school, club, or office—with people who also want to feel good about the relationship. Probably none of the people you relate to will put it in those terms, but that is what they expect from you if you want their commitment. Surely you have discovered that half a loaf is better than none, and half a loaf from a dozen or more people makes you a consistent winner. It is far better than a whole loaf from a person who is determined never to let you have another crumb in the future.

Accepting Personality Patterns

It is both your right and your responsibility to share the winnings with enough grace to allow people to feel good about themselves. To do this consistently, you not only have to apply the Law of Reciprocity, you have to use the Law of Economy as well. You must help people remain in their comfort zones as you work from an Accepting attitude that conveys the message that you are both worthwhile individuals in the relationship.

When negotiating, you have to remain true to your own pattern as well as accepting the patterns of others. It is crucial that you remain comfortable, because you will send out confusing signals, which are troubling, if you try to be something you are not. Your verbal and nonverbal communications will clash, and virtually everyone is disturbed by a person who sends messages that do not support each other. That is like facing a strange dog that is both barking and wagging its tail. You wonder which message to believe.

It is probably unnecessary to tell you to remain yourself, since most people do anyway, unless they are playing a role for some specific purpose. It is much more important for you to work at accepting people whose patterns are different from your own. An attempt to be something you are not comfortable being creates abnormal responses to you. In that case you will probably evaluate and make judgments of people who are not acting like they normally do, but who are reacting to your abnormal behavior. This is why many people have conflicts that they then cannot understand when they are comfortable once more.

Since you cannot change your pattern very much, except when you think about changing it rather than thinking about what you want to do or say, there are two things you can do. First, you can shift your pattern long enough to let someone become comfortable with you while rapport is being established. Second, you can work to let other people remain in their comfort zones without demanding that they conform to your unconscious expectations.

Last year my son and I called on a minister to whom we

hoped to sell a seminar program for his congregation. For reasons that we never discovered, we found the Comprehender pastor out of his comfort zone when we arrived. He was determined to get back to normal regardless of what we did or said, and we did not help him in time to save the relationship. As soon as he greeted us he retreated behind his massive desk as if it were a fortress wall, contrary to all principles taught in counseling classes. He watched us very analytically. When he said that our work could be valuable to his people, he turned and looked out the window. When he told my son how important young people were in his church, he toyed with a pencil and made tight, carefully controlled movements.

Too late in our interview, we decided that he was uncomfortable with my son's entertaining mannerisms and attitudes. At that point we tried to shift enough to establish rapport, but he had already made up his mind about our worth—and his conclusions weren't positive! He had become comfortable behind his fortress wall, but it was not a mutually beneficial meeting. Some of the members of the congregation, who are my friends and who had arranged the meeting, are critical of the way the man is unable to relate to anyone who does not meet his initial expectations. He has a history of moving frequently from charge to charge. If he would accept the fact that personality-pattern differences are normal, he could increase his effectiveness considerably in his ministry. And had we seen his needs earlier in our meeting with him, we might have developed the rapport needed to offer our program in his church.

Earlier I wrote that each person has a series of stereotypes that he uses to judge people according to the Law of Economy. Most stereotypes are based on whether people allow you to remain in your own comfort zone, however. Unfortunately, first impressions are crucial, and most people form them according to patterns with very little information about the trustworthiness, commitment, or expertise of the person being judged. They are formed almost instinctively, to remain comfortable, regardless of what happens to the relationship that affects the user's career, children, or happiness.

When you enter a new relationship or set out to persuade someone to do as you want, do so with an awareness of your stereotypes, which are much too centered on comfort. Learn to interpret patterns and the most common acts that go with them. That will enable you to establish the almost instant rapport that allows people to feel at ease with you. After that, when someone has accepted you as a comfortable person to be with, you can stop thinking about patterns and relating, as you will anyway, and get on with the issues at hand. By that time he has accepted you and is no longer forming initial impressions based on style rather than on substance.

Establishing a Rewarding Climate

The interpersonal climate you need in order to help people become aware of your ability and honesty is one that encourages authenticity and growth. Obviously, to anyone who has any experience in the real world, a large percentage of schools, churches, businesses, and families have climates that are not conducive to trust. That happens when the group members have been forced to accept the fact that only one person can be a winner there, that everyone else has to remain losers in the confrontations that occur regularly. Life is not really like that, however, for it isn't at all like a great football season where only the Superbowl winners have any status.

Such attitudes may have been valid in the past when life was grim and the only way to win rewards was to steal what other people had grown or built. Today, however, when wealth can be created by people who cooperate in their activities, the belief that only one person can win has little relationship to everyday life. Actually, I have no compelling desire to see you established in a Vail chalet if you keep me feeling resentful of you. If you have made me a friend, I may be able to appreciate your good fortune if you help me feel good about it.

When an adversary relationship has been created, people focus on their safety, spending a disproportionate amount of their time and energy in self-protection rather than in working toward a common goal. Such destructive relationships are common in many families when teenagers are trying to free themselves from the parental apron strings, as they must do to become self-directing adults.

Susan is a neighborhood girl my younger son dates from time to time. She is not especially eager to become a traditional housewife whose interests are limited to getting married, rearing a clutch of kids, and regressing with the coffee klatch until she falls apart when the nest is empty and her usefulness is past. She does, however, enjoy preparing gourmet meals for the family, providing they help her with the scut work after dinner is over. Last week she invited Jon in for dinner as she prepared an Oriental meal in her new electric wok. She insisted that her parents and guests let her manage the entire production. Unfortunately, her lack of experience caused a problem and the dinner was a failure. It was a potentially fertile field for her parents to humiliate her.

Because the home climate is a supportive one, however, Susan's parents treated it as a learning experience rather than a character failure. Her father joked with her and her mother invited everyone to the Dairy Queen for dessert after the kitchen had been cleaned. Susan's parents were demonstrating, with nonverbal communication, that they were supporting her creativity and independence. They would back her up regardless of complications that occurred because she was ambitious.

There are several things you can do to develop a mutually satisfying climate when cooperating with other people. You can establish rapport by getting them to talk freely about things that are important to them. After all, there are few people who can resist showing their winnings, even if they have no intention of giving them away. You can say:

> I saw in the paper that you entered the marathon again. What are your prospects this year?
>
> Alice Jones tells me that you were high in the balloting for teacher of the year. How do you win such commitment from your students?
>
> Is it true that you started your publishing business with a cookbook your wife compiled? How did you do that?
>
> Danny, you've had the car two nights this week. Now you tell me that you want it again. Can you tell me what's so important that you want to tie it up once more?
>
> I was talking to Mr. Kramer about the Midwest Wheat project and he said that you knew more about their finances than anyone in the company. Would you mind giving me a short summary of its importance to our plans?

These are questions that demonstrate your interest and turn people on because the topics are important to them. It is crucial that you ask such questions with the expectation of actually listening to the answer rather than simply using it as a ploy to manipulate the person, however. Since people have long since learned to interpret both verbal and nonverbal communication, your body language would reveal any impatience or boredom. Relax and listen as they tell you what is important to them.

You can also offer a sincere compliment to establish the beginnings of a cooperative climate. Once more you must relax and listen as you do your homework in advance, for everyone has been caught by people who use a compliment to manipulate them. Few things will destroy a developing relationship faster than an insincere compliment about an inconsequential matter. An effective compliment must deal with specific achievements rather than personality or character, as do the following.

> Mr. Harris, I've been impressed by the way you developed your marketing plan to sell sports-car bodies for old Volkswagens. The concept of advertising in men's magazines and then using a crew of telephone salespeople to sell large-ticket items was revolutionary. I take my hat off to you!

> Miss Anderson, you're probably wondering who I am. Don Howard is a friend of mine as well as yours. Last week at tennis he spoke so well of your program that I had to stop by. He told me that your work with retarded adults sends them back into society as contributing members. I'm fascinated and I'd like to do a story for the Sunday magazine. Could I ask you some questions about your work?

A statement intended to establish a cooperative climate that enables someone to be aware of your willingness to share the rewards must be sincere. It must also be pinpointed, as are the examples above, directly toward something the recipient is committed to. In other words, don't generalize. Go directly to an event you know is important. Don't tell a woman that her house is pretty if you are trying to interest her in volunteering for your election campaign. Do tell her how the colors and decorations blend to establish a warm, loving atmosphere for her and the family to enjoy. Such a compliment will virtually guarantee that she will at least listen to you. After all, you are showing good taste, since it coincides with her own! Such a perceptive person surely cannot be simply a manipulator.

Discovering Mutual Payoffs

In the opening chapter, I wrote that personal rewards are the basis of human motivation. As a result of that fact of life, you must discover what kind of reward each person wants for committing himself to your service. It isn't hard to find this out, but you'll have to stop assuming things about people without checking for verification. To do this you'll have to ask questions of the people you want to enlist. This means that you will have to abandon any Superiority charade—but, in any case, that would keep you out of the winning column.

One of the curious aspects of interpersonal relationships that Superiority players, manipulators, and losers fail to understand is that most people want to help others reach their goals. They want to do nice things for people who do nice things for them, according to the Basic Principle of motivation. Most people gain psychological rewards from seeing themselves as helpful individuals. And while no one wants to be the patsy who is manipulated into letting someone else leave with all the winnings, someone who feels good about another person is usually willing to let him share in the physical, psychological, or spiritual rewards of life. Since everyone has been hurt by manipulators, however, most people are careful not to become overextended until they are convinced that you are trustworthy. Developing a mutually supportive climate in which they become aware that you will allow them to maintain a good self-image and win appropriate rewards will enhance their awareness very quickly.

To help you identify the rewards that interest a person, you will have to become a behavioral detective, asking questions and sifting clues from the sands of verbal and nonverbal communication. Then you will have to give him what he will respond to, not what you want to get rid of. When the *Quincy* was sinking in World War II, a spellbinding snake-oil salesman could not have offered the four chaplains enough pleasure or prestige to corner the market on their life preservers. Something more was needed.

Admiral Rickover, who pioneered the use of atomic-powered submarines in the United States Navy, invested much of his time developing a group of highly competent young men for his program. Among them was Jimmy Carter. Since it was the most prestigious group in the Navy at the time, it had a flood of applicants, who had to be screened in short order.

During the selection process, Rickover would ask the youthful officers about their powers of persuasion. If a candidate admitted that he was persuasive, the admiral would create a scenario for the confident young man. He asked whether he could, aboard a sinking ship, be persuasive enough to talk a group of men into letting him have the only life preserver. If the young officer was foolish enough to say that he could, Rickover would open a door and four grim-faced men would enter carrying a life vest. Then the admiral would flash a frosty smile and tell the young man to start talking.

While an entrepreneur aboard the *Quincy* could not have purchased the lifesaving gear at any price, the four chaplains gave their preservers away to young men fighting their way up out of the engine room without any protection. They were living on the purpose level of life rather than the pleasure or power levels, as you will frequently have to do if you want to deal effectively with all kinds of people.

People select the rewards that lead to commitment for themselves, so you must discover what they want when you ask for cooperation. The best way to do this is to make them participants in your activities. I know of no better way than the technique used by Socrates with his students to make learning highly personal. As far as I know, he pioneered the technique of asking questions to help them discover answers that were deeply meaningful.

Allowing people to make their own choices is much better than using a multiple-choice approach, to say nothing of a solitary take-it-or-leave-it reward. You can identify desirable payoffs by asking questions that help people discover their needs in the relationship, see any problems that may arise, and find that being cooperative will remove some of the hindrances to meeting their needs.

If you are a supportive and empathetic person who uses his pattern effectively and avoids being manipulative, the greatest hindrance to winning interpersonal commitment is usually simple ignorance. This ignorance is often manifested by the use of unsubstantiated assumptions about the needs of others. Unless the assumptions upon which you base your persuasion are verified in some way, you will soon be in the position of the best horseshoe salesman in Chicago. No matter how perceptive, supportive, and accepting he becomes, he is not going to sell many horseshoes, for he is not meeting anyone's needs!

When I use a Socratic approach to test my assumptions and formulate more accurate ones, I politely inquire whether I may ask my intended collaborator a few questions about his life, job, or whatever is relevant. After I have established rapport, virtually everyone I have ever known will give me permission, for I transcend the standard manipulation model. Manipulators don't ask, they just tell! They tell people what to do to buy that chalet in Vail for them. I admit that once in a while I run into an outer-edge Comprehender who will have to think things over before he or she will give me permission.

In that case, when I see some hesitation or he asks why I want to question him, I always tell the truth. I say that I would like to understand him better and that a few questions will enable me to do so. Invariably, when I've established rapport before I ask for permission, my answer satisfies and I receive permission to continue. He realizes that I am not lecturing or being manipulative, so it is easy to start a dialogue. At that point, as he becomes a participant, he is half hooked already, for a Socratic dialogue is a powerful behavior shaper. It enables a user to talk himself into the most rewarding thing for him to do. I always start out with questions that deal with facts and are thus easy to answer. They can be:

> What classes have you signed up for this trimester?
> How many children do you still have at home?
> How do you and your husband both get to work with only one car?
> What day do you expect to reach Oregon?

Answers to these fact-oriented questions will enable you to get into his frame of reference, allow you to make better assumptions, and demonstrate that you are really interested in him as a person. The information will certainly help when you make your request as well.

Before long, however, you must move to a more complex set of issues that deal with motives and payoffs as he participates more fully in the dialogue. You must start asking questions that relate to the way he feels about life, his needs, and his expectations. The use of feeling-oriented questions will make it possible for you to test your assumptions about his needs and let you develop the desirable rewards that will win his commitment. Feeling questions can include:

> How do you and your husband feel about the Equal Rights Amendment?
> What do you think parents should offer their children in the way of education past high school?
> What would it mean to your life-style if you could double your income by working in my company?
> How would you feel about working to help people improve health care?
> What do you see as the most important aspect of your job?
> What would it mean to you if I could show you some rather simple ways to make your life more meaningful?

Such feeling-oriented questions cannot be answered by a simple answer, but require thought and continued interaction with you. They are both personal and important, but you have done something that few people ever do. You have given him permission to tell you what his feelings really are. In essence, your accepting attitude has told him that it's all right to disagree with you, as two intelligent adults sometimes do, without resorting to assaults on each other. In addition, the questions have created a new sense of expectancy, an anticipation of more to follow. He is in charge and telling you what is important to him as you appear, hopefully correctly, a perceptive individual who is intelligent enough to recognize his views. You have created productive tension, which can be resolved by doing something that should be done for his own good. He is being drawn deeper into participation, so that he feels that you are not doing something *to* him, but *with* him—and that's a tremendous difference.

Focusing Attention

Many people have no idea of how to win commitment from the people around them, so I suppose having low expectations makes little difference to them. Since it does for you, however, you will often find yourself in the position of persuading someone to do something worthwhile. Doing that can cause two kinds of tension. The first is relationship tension, which comes when people are not comfortable with each other. The second is task tension, which comes with the awareness that something *should* be done. Occasionally a person will decide that it is more comfortable to give up and do nothing than to relieve the tension in a creative way. In that case he may get rid of the tension-provoking element in his life—you! Be that as it may, you will often have to become quite specific in pointing out the danger potential in not doing what you want and the advantages to be found in cooperating with you.

When a person sees that his lack of rewards in a company is caused by discriminatory hiring practices, for example, he can do something that offers him a greater payoff. He can find a more rewarding place in which to work. If, on the other hand, he doesn't know why he has not been promoted, he may go through a number of trial-and-error learning experiences before discovering what his problem actually is. By using a Socratic dialogue, you can often help a person see his need or his problem more quickly and show him some solutions by visualizing what could happen if he worked with you.

When John Hendricks realized that his position as deputy superintendent for a middle-size city school district on the Pacific Coast was not going to lead him to the superintendency, he had no trouble making up his mind what to do. The superintendent, his boss, was a former big-college football coach who had returned to his hometown, where he had considerable political and personal power. He was just a few years older than John and showed no inclination to either leave in search of greener pastures or to die and thus leave the job vacant. Therefore, when John was offered the superintendency of a similar-size school district in another state, he accepted at once.

In a similar situation, another person might not be able to move as readily because of personal reasons which would block his doing so. Dan and Mary are both professors at the University of Wisconsin who are married and have a family in Milwaukee. Some time ago, Dan was offered the chairmanship of the chemistry department at a university in his hometown in New York State. Mary, however, in a tight teacher's market, was unable to find a suitable job at the school that wanted her husband. Dan did not even hint that she should give up her career to follow along in his wake. They did discuss the possibility of living apart for a few years, he in New York, she in Milwaukee, but that was not appealing to either of them and, besides, their children were on the point of armed rebellion at the thought. Dan regretfully refused the offer, for the rewards of chairing a department of his own were not as great as living with his children and his very talented wife.

You should make it plain to your friend that you are proposing an emotional partnership of some kind. The problems as well as the rewards will be shared as he gets full payment in coin of his own choosing, to the best of your ability to grant it. By this time, if you have followed the processes I've taught, you should be in the process of becoming a friend. After all, friendship includes such things as understanding, trust, empathy, and authenticity, and you have been demonstrating all of them in the relationship.

As you focus his attention on your willingness to share both problems and rewards, you can gain greater participation by summing up the facts and feelings he has revealed to you as you questioned him. The summation has been called the *Discovery Agreement* by Wilson, and it is very important to the relationship and to subsequent attempts at persuasion.

After I have established rapport, cleared away any lingering distrust, and identified his needs and problems, I sum all I have learned that is pertinent to our working together. The summation can be like this:

> Let me see if I understand you correctly. Feel free to tell me if I've gotten anything messed up. Okay? You tell me that the reason you've been cutting algebra is because Miss Thompson's down on boys who wear long hair? And you feel that no matter how hard you try she's going to give you a low grade? Is that what you're telling me?

If your son acknowledges that your summation is correct, the two of you have reached an understanding, a Discovery Agreement. You understand the problem as he sees it and he knows that you understand him, for you have put it into words that he agrees with. You also know why the reward of a good grade has no appeal any longer. He believes that a joker has been slipped in the deck to cheat him of his payoff. To get the reward he deserves, he will have to lose the payoff of being accepted by his shaggy-haired friends. And you know who is going to win that contest! You realize that he's not been smoking pot in the lavatory rather than attending class, planning to drop out of school and join the Marines, or doing something destructive. He is simply being deprived of his payoff due to the prejudices of a teacher.

Because of your Discovery Agreement, which has established your credibility, you can take steps to restore his reward for going to class. You can insist that he be transferred to another teacher, arrange for him to be permitted to drop the class and reschedule it the following semester, or confront the board of education with a lawyer, if nothing else works. The mutual Discovery Agreement makes it possible. Other Discovery Agreements can be:

> You're ready to leave the company because we've been bringing in new managers while neglecting to promote supervisors who have worked here for years? Is that what's troubling you? You feel that loyalty to the company has to be a two-way street and you doubt that it is? Is that why you want to leave?

> You're telling me that after working all day you're too tired to go dancing? That the effort leaves you too tired to sleep well and your work suffers the next day? Is that what you're telling me?

> Do I understand you to be saying that you need a larger income with your kids going off to school in the near future? That a regular eight-to-five job doesn't pay enough money for the education of your children? Do I understand you correctly?

Of course, such statements should be delivered in a low-key tone of voice to avoid sounding like a challenge. It should sound as if you are simply trying to get things organized in your mind because you are a friend and you want to understand what is troubling him. Understanding his motivation is of crucial importance to any subsequent negotiation or persuasion, for two reasons.

In the first place, you have focused the issue clearly in his mind. He may not have thought about it for some time, but he is certainly doing so now. Thus, you have also earned the right to make a recommendation when you have done this. Unless you have created rapport, questioned to clarify your assumptions, and summed your discoveries to his satisfaction, you have not paid your dues as a friend or, at the very least, as a supportive acquaintance. Your recommendations are still unverified assumptions and may be far from being a reward to him. And if he is a perceptive person, he will feel that you are simply asking him to buy you a chalet in Vail. If he has any intelligence, he will probably decline.

If, when you offer your summation, he tells you that you are wrong, all is not lost. Simply ask him to tell you how he sees the problem or need that you misinterpreted in your zeal to understand him more completely. If he is reluctant, smoothly and supportively continue to ask fact- and feeling-oriented questions until you understand him well enough to advance another summation. Then you will be in a position to recommend solutions that lead to mutual satisfaction, for they make sense to him now. You have created an interpersonal awareness that few people ever attain unless they spend weeks or months establishing rapport. You have established your credibility, demonstrated your understanding of him, and set the stage for a supportive relationship to continue.

CHAPTER EIGHT

Listening
and Persuasion

By now you should be aware of my contention that the success you gain by persuading people to cooperate with you is directly related to the interpersonal skills you use to reward them. You should also realize that interpersonal effectiveness is not an act that you perform, but a reflection of what you are. And one aspect of being an authentic person that others trust is to take a hint from the psychotherapist's training: to become a good listener. Indeed, few people ever become expert at listening, and that is a major problem. The importance of listening well, asking key questions, and encouraging men and women to answer without fear of being rejected or judged cannot be overemphasized. In fact, listening as a technique was difficult even for psychologists and psychiatrists to accept.

Freud pioneered the art of listening in psychoanalysis, but as his specific approach was subsequently modified because techniques evolved with the passing of time, the importance of listening as an instrument of discovery and assurance lost out to a more direct approach. For several decades, psychotherapists tried to work from a medical model of healing. They diagnosed and then recommended things for the patient to do. After all, if emotional distress and mental illness are diseases just like any others, telling people what to do to get well is the way to proceed, for the counselor or therapist is an expert with education, experience, and credentials to verify his expertise, while the patient is naïve and inept in matters of healing.

When a patient came for healing, the professional would order a battery of diagnostic tests, ask some routine questions, and then prescribe a course of action for the patient to follow. In other words, the therapists of that era did precisely what a physician would do as he diagnosed an illness and prescribed some appropriate medication. There was one slight difference, which soon became apparent to perceptive researchers in psychology and psychiatry, however. It didn't work! Men and women spent years in psychotherapy, after being diagnosed as having whatever names the American Psychiatric Association gave their problems, without getting any better. Directive counseling is a failure because there's a huge gap between what people know and what they feel. And knowing what the expert advised was a far cry from getting their emotions and behavior in order.

Eventually Rogers discovered that spending a week or so taking diagnostic tests at the beginning of psychotherapy was the worst start that a counselor could make, since it confirmed the sufferer's illusion that he was to deliver himself into the hands of a *healer* who would make him well. His expectations were wrong, for the only person who can cure an emotionally disturbed person is that individual himself. Accepting the medical model of leaving everything up to the expert usually sets a sufferer back for months or years before he learns that he must, in point of fact, heal himself.

One of the first breakthroughs in listening to the sufferer occurred when professionals realized that the patient wasn't really sick, because emotional distress is not a disease at all. It is a way of coping with life that has failed. It may lead to psychosomatic disorders, but it is not an illness in itself. In the second place, researchers learned that, regardless of his expertise, no professional worker can ever know a fraction of what his client knows about his emotions and behavior. Virtually all that any psychologist or psychiatrist can do is to help a client remain emotionally honest and sweat out his pain with him as he lays aside his immature ways of coping with life. The fact that some professionals still pretend that they are healers of the mind doesn't alter the fact that their clients heal themselves or else they do not get healed.

Some years ago a group of young white psychotherapists opened an inner-city clinic in a large Eastern city. Knowing that they were suspect by the largely black community, and being hopelessly understaffed, they recruited a group of intelligent young men and women from the community to work with them. The young assistants, who had been working at various jobs—as hairdressers, factory workers, and clerks—received a six-month course in client-oriented counseling techniques, in how to use community resources, and, especially, how to listen without letting their own egos get in the way. Then they were put to work in the community in which they grew up.

The results were astounding, especially to a professional who has spent from eight to ten years preparing to become an expert. They were able to establish rapport very quickly, could not be deceived by jive talk, and knew how to deal with the power structure of the community. In short, an evaluation of their work revealed that by using their listening skills, they functioned at least as effectively as the professionals with their training and experience. In some cases, the more empathetic of the young people were consistently more effective than the professionals.

Many people, especially those at the right of the pattern chart, have a tendency to talk before they listen. They advise before they know what the problem is or what the other person needs, often without realizing that knowledge is a dangerous gift, as a psychiatrist friend of mine discovered. When I was directing a Midwestern clinic, Andrew was one of our visiting seminar leaders for staff development. One day, when talking about using a directive approach, he said:

> I still have nightmares about a young man I so glibly advised to follow a course of action that seemed appropriate to me. He took my advice, for I was the expert, and step by step built upon my suggestion. My delusion that I knew what was best for his life brought about his death. It took him before a firing squad in Central America, where he and some friends were executed for taking part in a revolution. It was too late for me to help him, but I finally learned that the role of a psychiatrist is not the same as that of a physician.

Most recommendations are not so fatal, though I casually made the suggestion that directly led my brightest, most competent student assistant to take a sniper's bullet through his one-hundred-sixty-three-I.Q. brain in Vietnam. Advice without understanding is dangerous, and to understand another person you will need to listen with your ears, your eyes, and your body.

Mistakes Listeners Make

It seems as if our American mythology of Can-Do and straightforwardness has convinced many people that they are weak and ineffectual if they listen rather than talk, or ask for information instead of taking charge, whether they know what they are doing or not. As a result, many people blunder along through life never knowing what other people are thinking, but all the while assuming that they do. They fail to develop the introspective skills that would give them the insights needed to make better-quality, more acceptable recommendations. They also make mistakes that should not be made, since they are based on ignorance.

Through the years I have identified six common errors being committed by people who are poor listeners. You may find that some of them are keeping you from becoming as interpersonally effective as you would like to be. The most harmful ones are:

The criticizing listener. This person misses the point of many discussions, because he is more interested in form than in content. Often a Comprehender, he acts like a compulsive English teacher or speech teacher who automatically corrects people at dinner parties. Such a person picks facts and feelings to death because something in the situation does not meet his approval, so he sets people straight whether they want him to or not. He may also be a Superiority player who is meeting his distorted needs at the expense of others with his criticism.

The emotional listener. Some people, often Entertainers, become so involved with others that their perceptual screens keep them from learning the facts of the issue being considered when the facts contradict their assumptions. This happens frequently when other people reject our motives or manner with a negative statement or act. It can also occur when someone supports you with such enthusiasm that you don't hear the negative side of a plan or situation. This can lead to silly mistakes that an honest critic would have pointed out.

The distracted listener. Each person has many demands on his time and interest, so it is easy to have overloaded mental circuits. When you are distracted by the demands being made on you, normal concentration is impossible, and this is conveyed to the speaker in nonverbal ways, even if you murmur the polite words used in our society. A distracted listener often harms his own cause, because his distraction can be interpreted as a form of devaluation.

The factual listener. Facts are important, of course, if they support the flow of feelings that lead to commitment, even among Comprehenders and Controllers, who prefer not to express feelings openly. By themselves, however, facts often block interpersonal understanding and support, giving the impression that one is totaling the plusses and minuses like a computer that will then spit out a completely logical, unemotional decision. People do have trouble relating to a computer, however, and they will have trouble relating to you if you focus on facts the way a computer does.

The tangential listener. No one can focus constantly on a conversation or an idea for long without thinking about other things. The tangential listener, however, does more than that. He interjects his mental leapfrog into the situation in such a way that conversation rambles raggedly rather than moving smoothly toward a satisfying conclusion. It is especially hard for a logical Comprehender or an organized Controller to deal with such a person.

The pretending listener. Perhaps this is the worse mistake for an ambitious person to make when listening. It can happen from any of the personality patterns, of course, but impatient, competitive Controllers and Entertainers are frequently the culprits. They keep waiting for the speaker to draw a breath so they can tell how someone can buy them that chalet in Vail. In addition, he keeps making mistakes that reveal that he wasn't really listening.

Fortunately, for a person who wants to learn why people do the things they do, the human brain can function quicker than the tongue. Anyone can interpret information much faster than it can be presented by speaking. The difference in speed between speaking and hearing is so great that a skilled listener can both hear what he needs to know and plan a course of action during the pauses. Psychotherapists use a simple four-step technique that will be valuable for you as well. Here are the steps:

Analyze the input. Interpret what the speaker is saying

—or not saying, as the case may be. Does he focus on facts to the exclusion of feelings, or the other way around? Has he organized his materials, or is he shooting from the hip with assumptions? Why did he neglect to tell you something of importance to both of you?

Store the information. Reviewing the person's crucial facts and feelings mentally will give you a powerful instrument to be used later in the conversation. There is nothing you can do that will convince a person of your interest in him more than being able to quote him correctly at a later time. That demonstrates, without doubt, that you have, indeed, been interested in his needs.

Anticipate the future. Try to predict where he is taking the conversation and the points he will make. Ask yourself about the nature of the payoff he seems most likely to want. Aristotle used anticipation as a means of teaching his students to compare what was being said and what was actually happening. A mental application of contrast and comparison can help you anticipate what is going to occur in the future.

Speculate about possibilities. Few of the people you deal with will tell you all they feel. And some of them will not feel everything they tell you they do. You can help yourself by speculating about what is being said or what can happen if certain things happen. Speculating out loud once in a while allows you to capture his imagination with what can happen, while speculating silently lets you gain insights into why he fears you, will not talk, or tries to convince you with a flood of words that have no substance.

The common alternative to learning how to listen well is to overwhelm your prospective associate with a torrent of words and ideas in the hope that you can say something that will catch his interest. It will most likely lead to a terminal case of sensory overload—terminal to any hope of getting the understanding and help you are seeking, that is.

Listening to Learn

Everyone uses the process of selective perception when he is in conversation, lecture, class, or gathering of some kind. Obviously the ear mechanisms function as long as vibrations reach them, but not all the information is considered by the brain, for not all things are of equal importance. A person hears most clearly the sounds that have meaning to him. Surely you have experienced this at a party. You can be totally bemused by the buzz of conversation, the tinkle of glasses, and the background sound of music, which all seems to become a thick, heavy silence as you withdraw to your inner world. The voices and sounds continue, but you are miles away from it all, *until someone speaks your name*! Then you not only hear that, you also hear the sentence that preceded your name. You have chosen to interpret information that is important to you and to ignore the rest.

Choosing what you will respond to in a flow of conversation is equally important when persuading someone, for it will enable you to understand the needs, problems, and rewards that preoccupy the people you are trying to convince. Listening selectively enables you to predict which needs are important and which payoffs are acceptable.

Last month I was talking to Roger Reimer, who is a successful account executive in a Los Angeles advertising agency. I had visited him to discuss an advertising campaign my company was interested in conducting. When we discussed the nature of my Search for Meaning seminars, Roger became more than professionally interested, however. In fact, by listening to find out what his needs were, I soon pinpointed a deep sense of dissatisfaction with his life and work.

As our discussion continued, I sensed a deep longing for fulfillment and meaning which continued to elude him, despite his success in the business world. At that point I asked for permission to question him and soon discovered that he did not realize that a sense of purpose is vital to a meaningful life. Nor did he seem to realize that happiness is a by-product of having legitimate reasons for life to be satisfying. He had assumed that pleasure and affluence, as well as power and prestige, would be enough to make life fulfilling.

The longing I caught sight of was short-lived, as he quickly stifled his feelings and became professional once more. But because I had been listening to learn what I could about him selectively before I made my points clear, I gained an insight into his life that few of his talkative clients ever see. In fact, as I continued to listen, I revised my entire presentation in order to meet his needs for meaning and purpose more constructively. In the end, I had made a friend who is deeply committed to helping me produce a program that will help men and women move beyond the existential frustrations that are caused by an inadequate life-style. He has given me a commitment that just another advertising campaign would not have won.

As you listen to identify needs and predict acceptable rewards, select the facts and feelings that are related to your objectives, thus meeting your own needs and helping the speaker gain satisfaction by cooperating closely with you. Fortunately for people who wish to achieve a great deal, men and women constantly feel a gap between what they have and what they want, between what they do and what they want to do. It is this constant restlessness that makes a positive reward system effective. But the difference that leads to movement and growth must be discovered by listening to learn which needs and problems can be harnessed. Then you can start thinking about shaping your presentation of what the two of you can accomplish together.

Listening to Support

Conventional psychological wisdom states that people do what you want them to do for their reasons and not for yours. When I reward my younger son for mowing the lawn, he is doing what I want, but his reason is not the same as mine: to have a neat yard. He does it because he wants the money for a date or a movie. In addition, people don't cooperate because they understand what we want them to do so much as because they feel they are understood and accepted. If you have made him a friend by understanding and supporting him, he is likely to want to keep that psychological or spiritual payoff coming. This need for interpersonal acceptance is so strong that it can be used effectively in difficult situations. Professionals have learned that terrorists who hold airline passengers captive for political purposes become part of the group because a few days spent together create what is virtually a problem-solving unit. A terrorist who can shoot a guard or a pilot to capture an airliner finds it almost impossible to shoot half a dozen men and women he has come to know personally in the mutual experiences of the next few days. There are exceptions to this, of course, but it is so well established that anyone taken hostage shouldn't ignore the kidnappers, but should work at understanding and accepting their political motives as a means of building rapport.

To demonstrate your understanding of another person you can speed the process by doing and saying things he cannot misunderstand. Start by visualizing yourself in his place as you experience the joys, fears, expectations, and assumptions that relate to the situation. Work at convincing him that you feel these things with him. Use the technique taught with the Discovery Agreement in the previous chapter. Demonstrate superior understanding and accept-

ance by paraphrasing his facts, feelings, and statements to
the best of your ability. You can say:

> Let me see if I understand what you feel. You say that you
> would love to become an accountant rather than remaining a
> bookkeeper? Is that what I understand you to be saying? But
> your family obligations take all the money needed for tuition?
> Am I still on target? I can really understand how that would
> be frustrating to an ambitious woman like yourself.
>
> But what do you think you would feel if you came to work
> for me and I persuaded the boss to come up with a tuition
> grant so you could improve your worth to yourself and the
> company?

Such a statement demonstrates your understanding and
support beyond a doubt, and creates a surge of anticipation
and confidence. Simply paraphrase and ask if you are correct. Most of the time you will be, for you are restating
what he has told you, while being empathetic and supportive. But doing so makes you look like an interpersonal
genius, since no one else does so with him. Almost everyone
else just waits for him to stop talking so they can tell how
bad things are for them also. You are behaving in a unique
but supportive way, and it gives you an enormous influence
on the decisions people make.

Listening to Reward

Few people who have not studied psychology professionally
have any idea that a conversation and its outcome can be
shaped as deliberately as a sculptor shapes his clay. The
direction of a conversation can be determined by the use of
a few selective words interjected at appropriate times. Once
you have listened to learn what you can and have demonstrated your understanding supportively, you are in a position to reward a person for talking about his needs and the
rewards that will motivate him to help you.

Even the most doctrinaire Freudian psychiatrist, who professes belief in free-associating during which the client talks about anything he pleases, reinforces the conversation as he thinks it should go. A great deal of research taken from psychotherapy reveals that therapists of all schools use verbal and nonverbal payoffs both consciously and unconsciously. Positive rewards, as used with my colt Dandy and with Professor Davidson, are powerful change agents. Using short phrases and supportive gestures to reward people at the proper time helps to keep people moving along in a conversation. It is effective because we all need feedback in our relationships. A response gives a person a clue about his continued acceptance.

Even a compulsive talker like Johnny Carson or Carol Burnett will grow weary and will eventually end a monologue if all you do is sit silently as he babbles on. People need confirmation that all is well from time to time, as they discuss their feelings and needs. If the payoff is given randomly, however, the conversation frequently bounces about because of the random input, much like a loose football.

On the other hand, by waiting patiently and listening for an idea that is important to mutual goals, you can reward the key concepts and keep the speaker's focus on them as his students did with Davidson. This is an application of the Basic Principle, for you are doing good things when your speaker does. He talks about important issues and you give him emotional payoffs. To do this you have to remain an active listener rather than making the six mistakes I find common. But a reward encourages the speaker to move more deeply into subjects as an active participant—and that is what you want him to remain.

React positively only to those ideas that somehow connect with a decision to work effectively with you. Start in small steps, for a total commitment is too much to expect in return for a pleasant smile and a kind word. His momentum will increase as he becomes more deeply involved with you.

Imagine that you are counseling a student about poor study habits. If he complains about the ineptness of the administration and the poor quality of cafeteria food, remain respectfully silent even if you agree wholeheartedly on both counts. Agreement would only encourage him to speak more about ideas that are not important to the issue of his personal growth. If he speaks about the congestion in the parking lot, be noncommittal. When he mentions that he worked especially hard to complete a term paper, however, reward that statement about effort and excellence. Like Dandy, he will soon return for another payoff without your becoming directive and needing to tell him how he should behave and therefore creating a challenge to circumvent you.

Don't be too concerned about the conversation lagging while you are waiting for ideas you can reward. If you are accepting of the other person with your nonverbal communication, the silence of the situation will usually force him to find something to talk about. If you need them, you can use a number of focusing statements early in the conversation, then taper off and listen to what is being said. Eventually he will make a statement that can be reinforced to move the conversation in the appropriate direction. In addition to supportive words, you can use a smile, a nod, or a gesture to keep him talking long enough for you to find a place to reward the idea that cooperation will be mutually beneficial. You can shape virtually any conversation with the following rewards when you are both in your comfort zones.

> That's an interesting thing for you to say.
> Tell me more of your feelings about this.
> I see. Boy, do I see what you mean now!
> That's right on target, in my book.

I'm not sure that I understand. Tell me more.
I see that this is very important to you.
Great. Just great!
Can you give me an example?
Can you give me another example?

Any of these statements, as well as many more that you can think of, plus a smile, a nod, or an appreciative look, will guarantee his perception of you as a supportive person who deserves his honesty in return because you understand him so well. And given enough time and support, he will likely recognize the greater payoff he can win by working with you.

When some people are exposed to the concept of reinforcement for the first time, they mistakenly assume that it is too simple to be really valuable. Not so! In therapy and in my seminars, a few words placed at the appropriate time have worked marvels in changing attitudes and behavior. Nothing I have ever seen demonstrates this better than an experience I had in therapy with the wife of a friend.

David had come to me to force Suzanne into therapy because their marriage was falling apart. For several years she had been withdrawing more and more from the sexual intimacy which he took for granted. Until finally, before my meeting with David, she refused to make love to him at all. He was about fifty at the time and Suzanne was ten or twelve years younger. He had no intention of becoming celibate because his wife insisted he was a dirty old man to want sex after fifty. As he said, "I am *not through!*" Because her alternatives were either coming to me or getting a divorce, she came, but with little enthusiasm and no rapport. In fact, she had made up her mind, she told me later, to reveal none of her anxieties.

In our first session I spelled out the ground rules, dispelled the medical expectations so many clients come with, and asked her for any rules of her own. I said that all I could do was to help her face herself honestly, and to help her sweat out her growth from childlike defensiveness toward emotional maturity. My reluctant client sat silently for a moment and then spoke a few words about how distasteful the situation was to her. As she talked, I immediately rewarded her for saying something. As she responded to my acceptance, I told her that I could understand her feelings, that I would resent being blackmailed into visiting a therapist. Then I asked her if she would like to tell me about that resentment, in effect giving her permission to place the burden on her husband for demanding that she come and on me for acquiescing. That response took a few minutes. I then rewarded her for talking about concepts related to her marriage and her sexual experiences. Finally, I rewarded her both nonverbally and verbally (with a few words), to discuss her childhood sexual experiences.

In less time than I had spent with her husband, less than thirty minutes, the dam of more than twenty-five years burst and she poured out a story that was the source of her deep guilt and shame for decades. And she told it to the "busy-body" she had vowed less than an hour before never to tell a thing to!

At the age of fifteen, Suzanne had been sexually assaulted by her father, forced to have relations with him regularly, and put into an emotional double bind by her mother, who blamed her and defended the father. Finally, after several years, she stabbed him and fled. He did not die from the wound, but spent the remainder of his life in pain. Suzanne never spoke to either the father or the mother again.

At the age of twenty, she met David and married him without consciously realizing that his mannerisms and personality were similar to her father's. As their own children were reaching adolescence, however, her fears grew worse. She withdrew more and more, and her dissatisfaction increased. When her husband reached fifty, his resemblance to her father at the age she was assaulted was uncanny. Having sex with him was more than she could tolerate, considering her unrelieved burden of guilt and fear for her daughter. I'm happy to say that the story had a happy ending. The point of it is that by giving her simple verbal and nonverbal rewards as she talked, she told me things that her priest had never heard and of which her husband had no idea. The process is simple, but it is *not* simplistic.

The more effectively you reinforce a person for talking to you about important issues, the more he talks about them, the more involved he becomes, and the more likely he is to do something to increase his rewards. As he becomes an involved participant, the more likely he is to look for such a supportive and understanding person as yourself to point out the potential payoffs more clearly.

You cannot hope to persuade people if you dominate them and do not allow them to talk freely about their needs. The importance of listening in order to develop an accepting approach to managing behavior cannot be overemphasized, for men and women are determined to make up their own minds. Human beings have always been independent, but this trait is certainly more dominant today. People cannot discover all the advantages you are offering if your conversation keeps them from thinking about their problems and your payoffs.

Neither can you succeed by overwhelming others with logic or words, while allowing them to go from inconsequential rambling to redundancy and back again. Using the technique of reinforcement to lead them to the crucial issues when necessary keeps people focused where you want them. They will seldom realize what you are doing, but should they sense this, they will not resent it, because you are being far more understanding and supportive than anyone else they know. The majority of people will only perceive that you are a very rewarding person to talk to, someone who is remarkably understanding and who has the potential to be a real winner. Many may decide, at that point, to do as you want because they have been convinced of your ability to produce by the interpersonal rewards you have already given them.

One final word of caution: It is easy to let your own personality pattern *or* your prejudices interfere with your listening. Try to identify any ways by which you devalue people who are across the chart from yourself. See if you give verbal and nonverbal signs of rejection to members of the opposite sex, to people who are younger than you, or to those who are older. Of course, racial and religious differences are fertile grounds for people who need a Superiority illusion to feel good about themselves. Any such emotions will hamper your use of listening as a means of rewarding the people who help you.

CHAPTER NINE

Managing
Conflicts

Regardless of how well you understand motivation and how effectively you develop rapport and relate interpersonally, conflicts are bound to arise from time to time. Men and women get into trouble with each other because their personality patterns, assumptions, expectations, attitudes, and goals are incompatible in different areas of life. Sometimes conflicts are caused by simple selfishness, when one person or another insists on all the rewards for himself. In addition, thinkers as diverse as Sigmund Freud, Konrad Lorenz, and Saint Paul have concluded that human beings live in an unstable state of fear and distrust which complicates their attempts to live and work together peacefully.

Saint Paul called this unfortunate trait mankind's *carnal nature*, while Freud spoke about the *id*. Lorenz attributed our propensity toward conflict and violence to a need to defend our physical and psychological territory from those who would encroach upon it. It is obvious that they and others were writing about the same condition of humankind. There does seem to be a deep stratum of *homo-sapiens anger* which was probably internalized as a result of the race's terrifying experiences as fangless, thin-skinned little creatures who were imaginative enough to picture what could happen to them as they were competing for survival on the African savannah.

Regardless of how the race's propensity for conflict and violence developed, it is hard to account for the sheer ferocity humans have displayed in this century alone without assuming that certain destructive tendencies are an inherent part of human nature. In that case, you will need to let sleeping fears remain undisturbed and learn how to cope with the anxieties that well up from deep in the human unconscious to trigger the conflicts that trouble all human relationships to some degree.

Reassuring Anxious People

The advocates of winning through the use of power or intimidation made their recommendations without reference to fear or anger. Neither Ringer nor Korda considered either emotion in their books. That, in itself, would make their recommendations suspect to me, because, as a result of conducting thousands of hours of therapy, I have found that fear is a major cause of much violence and conflict.

After a speaking engagement in which I talked about the relationship between fear and violence, a man came to see me. Harold Larsen said:

> I've always thought of myself as a self-controlled, logical Dane, but something happened last summer that revealed my vulnerability to irrational fear. Toward the middle of July a stray cat found her way into our basement to have a litter of kittens. They were born dead, so I disposed of them and chased her away. But she kept coming back to look for them when the kids left the door into the garage open, calling piteously, and finally making a nest for herself behind the food freezer where no one could reach her.
>
> To get rid of her I made a noose from a cord and a coat hanger, with the intention of leading her out and really laying down the law about the door being left open. As I started down the stairs, my wife casually mentioned that she hoped

the stray didn't have rabies or something. I went into instant shock, but being a real macho type I had to go on with my grand safari instead of leaving the door open and shutting her out when she left for food or water.

I went quietly to the freezer, found her asleep, and slipped the noose over her head. I had no intention of hurting her, for I am very fond of cats, but she panicked and so did I. She struggled to get free and I tightened the noose, for I certainly didn't want a rabid cat clawing her way up my arm to my jugular vein! The little creature retched a few times and went limp, for I was choking her to death. I realized that I was holding her like I had a thousand-pound steer on a line. I even considered killing her on the spot so she couldn't ravage me when I turned her loose, telling myself that I could claim an accident. Then I relaxed, carried her outside, and released her, frightened but unharmed.

The thing that troubled me, however, was the way I became murderous because I was afraid. So I dug back into my childhood to find why I was violent. When I was a kid on the farm, a neighboring farmer contracted rabies by washing out a horse trough with a cut hand after a horse had been bitten by a rabid squirrel. By the time he learned the cause of his illness he was beyond treatment and died a horrible death that shocked the community. All that fear came welling back when my wife said what she did. And I fought for my life! Is that why we humans have so much conflict, to keep from getting hurt?

Harold was right, according to Bonaro Overstreet, who writes that fear is what a person feels when confronted by a real or assumed danger. She also wrote that fear is a very complex emotion for men and women, often leading to attacks and consequences that they do not understand. People typically react to danger and the fear it produces by fighting to survive or by fleeing for the same reason. Today, however, in all but the most primitive relationships, either fight or flight causes more problems than it solves. A frightened person may flee the benefits you want to share with him. Or he or she may attack your judgment out of fear that you are being deceptive. And obviously you cannot resolve the tension or stress being felt, when forced from your comfort zone, by running screaming from your office or by smacking the boss smartly alongside the head. The immediate relief gained by either course of action would soon be followed by more anxiety in a very short while.

Fear, which may be of either a physical or a psychological nature, will be the major reason why men and women refuse to cooperate with you when it is in their best interests to do so. They may fear losing the rewards you promise. They also may fear financial loss, or feeling badly about themselves, or looking like a dunce to people who might call them foolish. The fears and angers that lie just below the surface of consciousness are like a basket of snakes, and you will have to account for them in your attempts to negotiate and persuade.

Assuming that a person is not emotionally disturbed, however, he can overcome this fear and anxiety if you remain understanding and use some techniques from psychotherapy. You must assure him that his cooperation in what you are requesting will not cause him pain because you are, indeed, a sincere and competent person who is in a position to help him feel better about himself.

Much resistance can be reduced by dealing openly with the concepts that frighten him and could possibly lead to conflict. There is no better way than to follow the three steps given below.

1. Accept and support his right to feel fear.
2. Formulate and confirm a question about it.
3. Answer the question to his satisfaction.

Comprehenders and Controllers have a tendency to ignore the importance of fear and anxiety, because they focus on self-control rather than on self-expression. On the other hand, Supporters and Entertainers tend to make too many decisions based on emotions when they'd be better off considering some facts. Whatever your pattern, however, or the pattern of the person who needs assurance, you must start by accepting his fear as real, especially when he is out of his comfort zone.

Accept his emotions by admitting that his feelings are reasonable and not unusual under the circumstances. By doing this you will cause him to think more clearly about the payoff you are offering, and you will demonstrate that you really do understand him. It will also help steer him away from an either/or choice for which he is not ready. Obviously, if you refuse to accept a person's fears as important, he will think that you are questioning his intelligence or his emotional stability. In that case you will have destroyed any rapport you have developed. Express your acceptance and support of his resistance or fear by saying something like the following:

> I can see why you feel that way under the circumstances.
> I appreciate your concern with that point.
> That's an interesting issue, isn't it?
> If I were in your place, I'd feel about the same way.

The next step is to turn his resistance or fear into a request for additional information. In a majority of cases I find that an objection is actually such a request, though you often have to make him aware of it. You can help him realize that he needs more information, while accepting his feelings, by saying:

> You've brought up a crucial question.
> I think I understand your question better now.
> That's a very perceptive question.
> That's a question other people have asked me.

If he doesn't stop you to deny that he's asking a question, you can continue to say:

1.   As I see it, your question is, "Will your coming to work for me give you the money and job security you want?" Is that your real concern?

2.   As I think about your question it seems to me that you are asking, "Why should I go to college when so many graduates have to work at jobs that have nothing to do with their degrees?" Is that what you really want an answer to?

3.   It seems to me that your basic question is this: "If you work in Don's campaign, how can you be sure you'll have input into his policies after he's been elected?" Is that your real question?

Naturally you should answer the question you have brought into focus for him. You must remain perceptive enough at that time to interpret his nonverbal signs as well as what he has to say. And even if he rejects your attempt to focus his interest by stating that you have missed the mark, you have not reduced his trust in any way. You are still being supportive and accepting, just the way an interpersonal expert should be. You can openly ask him to tell you what *is* bothering him, what his question *really* is. Doing so gives him permission to be honest with you, something that few people ever do, though they pretend to. In such a unique setting he may just tell you the truth!

To reassure him about the reward you are offering, a short story about someone who benefited in a similar situation can be used, pointing out what happened to them, with the words *feel, felt,* and *found,* as Wilson suggested.

I understand how you *feel* about collecting for the Community Chest campaign. Quite a few people tell me how they *feel* embarrassed asking others for money.

Donna Harlengen *felt* much the same way. She was worried that working for the campaign would make her look like a public beggar to the neighbors and take too much time from her job.

After Donna got into it, however, she *found* it to be a great source of satisfaction. Her kids pitched in and her husband fixed dinner on those evenings she was out helping take pledges for people who need help. She *found* the personal satisfaction so great that she's signed up for this year also.

Of course, if you've gotten your intended cooperator to agree to a question as troubling him, you should answer it to his satisfaction. You could answer the three questions given above by saying:

1. I understand why you're concerned about changing jobs. Jim Wilson felt the same way when I persuaded him to come help me on another project. Today he manages a group that's doing more than a million dollars in business each year. He's largely his own boss and does his work his own way. He's set for years and we promote from within the company. He's making more than fifty thousand with bonuses and overrides, which is more than twice what his last job paid him. Does that answer your question?

2. I see what you're driving at. How can you be sure that you'll be able to find a job after spending four years in college? That *is* enough to make you think seriously, isn't it? I've done some research that may answer your question, however. If you choose a degree in accounting, engineering, sales, or marketing, you'll have no problem finding a job at a good salary. Does that answer your question?

3. Of course, I see why you should be concerned. Who would want to be used and then forgotten? Julia Shields worried about that in Don's first campaign for the school board. When he won a seat, he set up a parent's advisory group to make recommendations to him. Julia's still the chairwoman and she's working for Don in this election also. Does that answer your question?

Conflict Avoidance

Any person can avoid conflict at almost any time. All he must do is avoid having opinions, surrender to the demands made upon him, and become a robot who obeys as programmed at all times. Since few people want to live that way, and since the pressures generated by our current life-style are great, conflicts continue to complicate relationships, because few people know how to handle them with the Law of Reciprocity. A good conflict-avoidance technique, such as this, allows you to come away with the half a loaf that is your key to consistent winning. It enables both people to remain in their comfort zones and to avoid the stress that leads to immature behavior.

This technique, first suggested by Ginott, will not help a great deal if you are fighting to keep your job when the boss's cousin has his sights set on it. In that case you will have to fight for survival rather than negotiate with him. The same is true if someone is contemplating a course of action that is detrimental to the well-being of your family, school, church, or company. In that case, half a loaf may be too much of a compromise to make. In most situations, however, conflicts are less noble. Most of them occur when frustration is high and you are looking for ways to find relief. No great issues are present, so you can gain acceptance and support with the Law of Reciprocity rather than resentment and resistance with the Law of the Jungle. The technique is based on the fact that all your feelings are legitimate and necessary for survival.

Deep-seated emotions are normal, though their expression is not always appropriate. The fear that a worker feels when told that his job will be automated is totally logical. Sexual feelings keep the race with a supply of children as well as binding men and women together in a permanent home, which is needed to give children the stability they need. Anger, which is directed at someone who is monopolizing all the rewards by making you look bad to your boss, is justifiable. So is hatred of anyone who assaults you physically or psychologically.

Because all normal people feel the same kind of emotions you do, the vast majority of people will accept your right to have them, provided that you do not attack them personally as a means of feeling better at their expense.

Anne, who is a kindly-appearing Supporter, had planned a staff meeting at which one of her employees was scheduled to report to her staff. The meeting was important to the group, so she had planned on her supervisors discussing the ramifications of a certain problem and reaching a decision before the meeting was over.

Peter, the young research assistant, failed, however, to arrive on time. He had planned poorly, stopping to gather additional data. Anne was furious with him, because she felt that there was no point to holding the meeting in his absence.

As time passed and the meeting rambled on to a fruitless conclusion, Anne was no longer in her comfort zone. By the time Peter arrived with his information, she was deeply disturbed by what had happened. When she spoke to Peter about her displeasure, he failed to respond with any show of contrition, because he is a Comprehender. He simply told her that he had not been satisfied with the data he had and that it was better to present nothing than an incomplete report.

At that point Anne made the mistake that many Supporters do. Rather than confront him, she acquiesced to keep the relationship pleasant. Unfortunately, this told Peter that she was no more concerned with schedules then he, and that she wanted the same degree of perfection. Actually, promptness was very important to her.

Later Peter failed Anne again and she did not tell him what she felt about the delays he was causing. Finally, when his need for even more certainty in his research caused her to look bad before her boss, she slipped from the tension level to one of stress and attacked him bitterly, as Supporters do at the second level of frustration. She attacked his personality, his attitudes, his motivation, and his commitment to the company.

Her research assistant, who was actually very thorough

and valuable, was stunned and deeply hurt by her attack, for he had assumed that Anne felt as he did. He had mistaken her acquiescence for agreement; therefore, the attack seemed petty and irrational to him. As a result of being out of his comfort zone, he tried to avoid her, and when that failed (she continued to attack), he became autocratic and told her that it was her own fault because she was a poor manager. In a few weeks he found another job and left her to ponder what had happened.

Anne could have handled the situation effectively by using the Conflict Avoidance Technique as a three-stage process. In the first instance, rather than acquiescing, she should have remained authentic, telling what she felt by saying:

> When I plan a meeting and I don't have you here to support me with whatever data you have, I feel like I'm not getting the help I need. It bothers me so much that I'd prefer half the information to none. We can adjust to additions later.

If Peter listens to her, as most people will if allowed to remain in their comfort zone, he will probably see her point and cooperate as expected. They will have come to an understanding about something in the relationship that troubles her. If, however, he fails to accept her requests, she has both the right and the responsibility to increase the intensity of her feelings the next time he lets her down. In the second stage of the Conflict Avoidance Technique, she should increase the intensity to say:

> When you take so much time perfecting your work that I don't have information when I need it and look ineffective to others, I become very upset. I feel that I'm not getting the cooperation I need and that disturbs me, since you have much to offer this department if we can get our work synchronized.

If Peter has a normal level of intelligence, he ought to get the message about her need for him to move faster than he has done. Unfortunately some people have such a thick perceptual screen, or such Superiority attitudes, that they don't hear things that trouble them, or else they feel that change is impossible. If Peter still does not cooperate, Anne should go on to stage three, though she must realize that it is virtually an ultimatum that can end the relationship if he cannot or will not change. She should say:

> When you do not consider the overall needs of the department, I feel a great deal of frustration and anger with you. It upsets me so much that I put pressure on people who do not deserve it. In short, should this take place again, I'm going to put a note in your file that no annual raise will be considered. That's how furious I become when your delays make me look bad as a manager.

Peter would have no doubts about his standing with Anne at this point if she had been authentic with him, and she would have remained in her comfort zone to deal with the issue as an adult, instead of with deep frustration. Notice, however, that in the example she never assaulted his character or his motives. She focused almost entirely on her own feelings, which is a legitimate thing to do. She allowed him to remain in his comfort zone in all three stages of the process and gained enough symbolic relief to remain comfortable herself. Since she is not attacking his character, he need not become defensive. They could then solve the problem by negotiating a compromise between his need for certainty and her need for action.

Conflict Control

The more demanding or intense a relationship, the more likely the chance of conflicts arising. Actually, any good manager wants his assistants competing for his job when he is promoted. A teacher wants students to strive for knowledge and skill, while parents want their children to mature to self-control and achievement. In spite of the desire for appropriate competition, however, few raw conflicts are productive. Most of them cause emotional distress, which lowers commitment and dedication. Fortunately many conflicts can be stopped with another technique if they are caught before the participants have been forced too far from their comfort zone. For one perceptive teacher and his student, it happened like this.

Carlo had been teaching music in high school for quite some time. He was good and demanded the best from the student musicians. As a result, he had a long record of winning competitions and contests across the region. He had learned how to use the Conflict Control Technique in a seminar I had conducted for teachers earlier. He used his knowledge one afternoon when one of his students confronted him after missing the bus to a football game. The steps of the Conflict Control Technique include:

> *Accept the speaker's complaint without rejection.* Be an active listener who really hears what the speaker's words convey.
> *Share the speaker's concern by agreeing and sympathizing.* You can say, "I see what you mean," or "If I were in your place, I'd feel about the same way."
> *Reflect the speaker's feelings to demonstrate understanding.* You can paraphrase his statements after saying something like, "Let's see if I understand what you are saying."
> *Advocate new information to help him change his mind.* He needs a logical reason to agree with you, so offer one that will keep him from seeming indecisive.
> *Confirm his agreement by asking for acceptance.* Get him to commit himself verbally, to close the issue on a positive note.

Accepting, sharing, and reflecting deal with the angry person's emotions. The three steps allow him to gain relief by returning to his comfort zone. After this happens, he can more effectively deal with facts in the two final steps—ad-

vocating and confirming. The method most people use re-
verses the order of dealing with facts first and emotions
later, if at all.

The angry youngster ran up to Carlo, after the band bus
had pulled away, to shout:

(Accept)
Jack: Why did you let the bus leave without me? You said
you'd put my name on the list at practice this morning. It
really burns me up that I missed the trip because I was busy
in shop.

(Share)
Carlo: Boy, oh boy! Did I ever goof. I must have missed you
in the confusion. You must be furious. And I admit that I'd
be as angry as you, if it had happened to me.

(Accept)
Jack: It's more than the game and the trip. I made plans to
meet a girl at Southwest High. She's really nice and she's expecting me. That's worse than anything else.

(Reflect)
Carlo: You had plans for a big date, and I messed them up by
forgetting to put your name on the list. That's really bad, and
I'm sorry for ruining the date and all.

(Accept)
Jack: Yeah!

(Advocate)
Carlo: The driver had a tight schedule, so he left right on the
dot, and I overlooked you when some sophomores started
quarreling over window seats. But let's try this. Why don't
we see if you can get a ride with one of the teachers? Someone usually drives to the game. I'm not going myself, for I
have to practice for a concert this afternoon, but someone
may.

Jack: You think there's a chance?

(Confirm)
Carlo: I don't know, but let's go to the office and find out.
I'll do my best to help you find a ride. I can't promise any-
thing, but I'll try. Oh, will you forgive me for being careless?

Jack: Uh, oh yeah! Let's go check. And I—uh, guess I

could have kept a closer watch on time and swept the shop a little sooner. It's probably my fault as much as yours.

Even if a ride cannot be found, the technique allows Carlo to maintain rapport much better than a brusque denial of responsibility. Jack responded as Carlo did and the conflict was ended. If the teacher had not been partially to blame, the process would still help the youngster feel better about himself and less like an adversary in the relationship. Even when it is not possible to find a compromise or to grant partial fulfillment, understanding and acceptance can be maintained.

Supportive Refusal

When solutions are not negotiable and you have to require cooperation or compliance, it can still be done in such a way that good relationships can continue. As in many cases, it is not so much what you do, but how you do it. This is effective because most people prefer a mutually supportive relationship to winning all the payoffs. Offering support when an occasional payoff must be withheld will keep the relationship strong. Obviously you cannot use the refusal technique too often, or it will lose its effectiveness because the payoffs are out of balance. The five steps of the Supportive Refusal Technique are:

> Accept the person's request in supportive terms.
> Express understanding by paraphrasing the request.
> State the legitimate denial in authentic terms.
> Help the person be authentic about his feelings.
> Restate the denial firmly but supportively.

Acceptance, as it always does, enables another person to gain emotional relief without receiving interruption or rebuttal, which would devalue him. After he has been encouraged to say what he feels, you should then speak supportively. You could say:

I know how badly you wanted the Seattle assignment. It would have been perfect for you and your family.

Expressing understanding is best done by putting his feelings into your own words to demonstrate that you know how he really feels.

You've done a great job with your division. I know that! In fact, your ability is why I need you here for another year. With the Midcontinent contract, I can't get along without you in my corner.

In a different situation you could say:

I know you've been quite successful and will be even more so in the future. That's why I want to keep you here to speed your growth, instead of sending you to the West Coast. The experience you'll get with John and myself for another year will pay off for your career in the long run. I'll see to that.

Stating the denial with authentic words and body language will give him something to reason about once you have accepted and supported his emotions. You could say:

You must remain here for another year rather than taking charge of the Northwest District. You are too valuable to me under the circumstances.

Helping the disappointed person express his feelings clears the air and offers more symbolic relief.

You probably feel like I'm playing the boss in an arbitrary fashion. That's your right to have such feelings, and if I were in your place I'd feel some resentment also. It's too bad that we can't always have things work out the way we want. We work so hard and things sometimes don't break the way we hoped. Life sure makes me feel angry and resentful at times. But we'll have a great year with the Midcontinent business. You'll understand before it's over.

Restating the denial in a firm but noncritical manner helps gain acceptance and close the issue permanently.

You're needed here if we are going to do our best with the

new contract. When we're on top of that situation, in a year or so, I'll see that you run your own show. In the long run we'll all profit more from your loyalty and effort here this year. I'm sure that you, of all people, understand that. Feel free to call on me for support any time you need to during the coming year. I'm counting on your expertise and enthusiasm to get us through. All right? Let's keep in close touch about our work.

The Supportive Refusal Technique forms a clear, logical answer to a disappointed or angry person with whom you cannot negotiate the outcome except to give him support and acceptance. It takes very little more time than a curt refusal, but it speaks volumes about your concern for his feelings. It also avoids the weaknesses of a long, unstructured discussion, for it touches the critical emotional issues.

Most of the refusals that complicate your attempts to include men and women in mutual payoffs will occur because people are afraid of getting hurt. Fear not only makes people flee from you, it also makes them fight. Even many situations that look like blatant selfishness usually result from someone's fear of not getting what he deserves for his investment of time, money, or self.

Spend time reassuring people who are in doubt of your willingness or ability to share the rewards of life with them. Avoid conflicts without surrendering, and control those that are started in spite of your best efforts. Finally, refuse unacceptable requests in such a way that an interpersonal payoff is substituted for the tangible one. You will find, as you do these things, that life will become a peaceful, largely conflict-free experience.

PART THREE

Winning
Consistently
(Offering Satisfying Rewards)

CHAPTER TEN

Offering
Winning Options

Most unsuccessful attempts at persuasion fail for one basic reason: They do not come to grips with the emotions that undergird virtually all cooperative ventures. The typical person who tries to persuade others deals with dates, times, products, colors, profits, and so on, without relating these facts to how cooperation will make the committed person feel. This is true for people in all sectors of the personality-pattern chart, for those who conceal their emotions still feel as deeply as those who express them openly. And the people at the bottom of the chart, though they are more comfortable talking about emotions, seldom know how to harness their use of feelings to draw the mental images that persuade other people to help them.

People aren't won to a cause because of pleasure, money, fame, or power as often as we usually assume. They offer their commitment to someone who has shown them that doing so will meet certain needs or remove specific problems. In other words, we can safely say that people will do what you ask them to because of the way you make them feel about an important issue. They do as you ask for their own private reasons, to feel good about them-

189

selves, about their possessions, about the relationship with you, or about life in general.

To effectively persuade people, you need to follow the general, three-phase progression that has been included in the preceding two parts of *Nice Guys Finish First*. You must:

1. Relate warmly and supportively.
2. Discover problems and needs.
3. Reward satisfying payoffs.

A section of the book has been devoted to each of the three relationships that lead to interpersonal commitment. And it is probably obvious that the length of each of the three sections is related to the importance of each aspect of winning.

Relating warmly and supportively establishes a cooperative climate in which other people realize that you are a friend who can be trusted. In fact, if you have not used your pattern and the techniques presented to become a friend, the rewards he demands in return for his commitment may likely be greater than you can grant.

The section about the discovery of needs and problems by creating awareness, by listening, and by coping with conflict is shorter, because a healthy interpersonal climate has been established for the supportive relationship and its dialogue to continue. Both preceding sections set the stage for offering choices that are pinpointed to needs and problems.

In this last section, the actual suggestion that he or she work with you to win consistent payoffs from life is rather simple and straightforward, *after* you have created the cooperative climate and discovered what he is going to want from the relationship. Only then are you knowledgeable enough to make recommendations that make sense to him, for you have demonstrated that you are a perceptive, supportive friend who can offer suggestions that will really help. Therefore, this last section of *Nice Guys Finish First* is rather short. The crucial work has already been completed before you reach this point.

Making Recommendations

The solutions you suggest must come after the Discovery Agreement, for not until then have you learned enough about his needs and sufficiently convinced him of your understanding to win his acceptance of you as a perceptive friend. In fact, up to the time that you recommend a solution, he may not even realize that you are going to do so, if you have used these interpersonal skills well. When you have related acceptingly and used your skills to listen as you shape the conversation, your solution will sound like a benevolent afterthought rather than the point of the entire conversation. It will be all the more effective because it seems spontaneous.

The discovery aspect of the relationship should have created tension for him as he became more deeply aware of his need or problem that should be resolved. In fact, knowing that one should do something within a certain length of time is as good a definition of tension as I have ever heard. Furthermore, he knows that you understand his need, because it was discussed in the Discovery Agreement. This tension puts him in the position of wanting to resolve it to return to a state of satisfaction. It is at this point, when awareness, understanding, and tension come together, that a sensible recommendation will be most acceptable. You can lead him to make a decision by saying:

> From what you've told me, Jerry, it seems that you could make the contributions to society that are important to you *and* offer a better life-style to your family by coming to work with me.

In view of what our discussion has revealed, it sounds like a young woman with your skills and interests should consider a science or technical career.

Based on what we've found out as we've talked, you could resolve this problem by getting enough sleep so that you could get to work on time.

Your suggested solution thus seems the most logical, normal thing he could do under the circumstances. And if he does not accept it at this point it is probably because you have failed to maintain trust, because you have misinterpreted his needs, or because he has decided that doing as you recommend is the lesser of the payoffs he is seeking. There are three aspects of what he will enjoy if he cooperates with you. They are:

1. The resolution of the problem
2. The advantages that will accrue
3. The rewards he will enjoy

He can resolve the problem identified in the Discovery Agreement by following your recommendation. This is the straightforward nuts-and-bolts solution that makes sense, whether or not he accepts it. You tell him that a year invested in a technical school would make him employable, that an end to his macho games with a sensitive wife will end her resistance to his sexual advances, or that working part-time to restore the shattered family budget will make a vacation possible next summer.

Recommending a solution does two things. It tells him what is expected, so no unpleasant surprises crop up later as you tell him about the terms on which the relationship will prosper. You can also briefly elaborate upon the duties of the job, the household help you need, the depth of commitment desired from a tutor of retarded children, and so on.

The advantages are the factual benefits he will gain by

doing as you recommend. Some kind of transition should be made from the resolution of his problem to the advantages he will gain by doing as you suggest, however. The easiest kind of transition is a sentence or two like the following:

> You'll find working here rewarding because we really practice what we preach about participatory management.
>
> When you help one of our kids learn a skill, you're helping him become a contributing member of society.
>
> The key factor in working for the committee is that it will give you a real voice on the city council.
>
> When you help me do the housework, you can expect me to have more time for the things we enjoy doing together.

The advantage you point out is what will happen when he cooperates. It shows how his needs will be met or his problems solved. You can use examples, anecdotes, charts, or anything that will be convincing. I find that a story about someone else who gained the advantage I am offering is very helpful. Something like the following is quite effective.

> Using our data research program means that when you need a map of your lagging customers, you can punch up a request and every salesperson will have the information on his territory in a chart form. Dan Hughes at InterCity Sales uses it, and he told me how it keeps his people on top of their customers' latest purchases with no wasted time.
>
> If you'll stop cutting classes and study ten hours a week, you'll get to spend the summer with your cousins in San Diego, as you want to.

Describing the advantages of cooperating in a specific manner tells precisely how his need is met. It is what he can expect as he resolves his problem in a manner that he can understand. It is doubly effective because you have pinpointed it precisely from your preceding conversation. If at all possible, you want to demonstrate the advantages of cooperation in some tangible manner. After all, many people since Confucius have correctly said that one picture is worth a thousand words. A confirming phone call to a satisfied customer, the payroll records of a successful salesman, a diagram of tasks for a new worker, a supportive letter from your sister in San Diego about the summer of surfing, are all powerful persuaders at a time of decision. The use of tangible aids is even more important if you are offering intangible advantages, for they will help him see them in his mind's eye. Use graphs, charts, paintings, or whatever is necessary to make your point.

One thoughtful father persuaded his son to remain in college by listening well and writing two checks for the young man. Chris was determined to drop out of college in his junior year to take a job as a skiing instructor in the mountains above Salt Lake City. He told of all the fun he would have as Carl listened carefully. When the boy's enthusiasm leveled off, the father tried to convince him of the advantages an education would give him, but to no avail. Chris was simply too wrapped up in the excitement of his plans, though he did admit that he would be living at a subsistence level for several years, until he developed a clientele on the slopes. Carl heard his son saying that money was going to be a problem, however, because he was actually listening rather than simply focusing on his own arguments.

When the conversation lagged, the father took his checkbook from his jacket and wrote two checks to his son. One was made out for two hundred fifty thousand dollars. He handed it to Chris and said:

> This is what you can expect to earn in the next thirty years without a degree in a salable field. It looks like a lot of money, doesn't it?

The father then took the other check, filled out for half a million dollars, and pushed it to his son. Carl said:

> This is what you'll have to share with your family if you finish
> your degree and work for the next thirty years. Can you really
> ask your future wife and kids to make that kind of sacrifice so
> you can have an extra few months of skiing?

Chris sat quietly for a few minutes and then agreed to postpone his working as a ski instructor until after he graduated some eighteen months later. He later admitted that he could not get the difference in earnings out of his mind. The visual impact was simply too great.

Finally, you must spell out how the reward will be enjoyed. You can talk about the feelings he will have about himself when he resolves his problem and gains the advantage the way you suggest. His own self-image is crucial at this point, as well as the respect and support of his peers. You should clarify how cooperating will make him feel good because he is having fun with you, developing a career, being useful in life, or finding meaning and fulfillment in a new manner. He will have less worry, find deeper satisfaction, or have more friends as a result of what has happened. Be sophisticated in your recommendations, however.

Don't ask a prospective employee if he wants to come to work for you. Ask him whether he would like to make a new start in a business that rewards and promotes on merit alone. Always take time to tell him how he will feel when he resolves his problems and meets his needs. This is the personal reward that will move him toward commitment, yet it is the one most often neglected when asking for help.

Ask a housewife how she would feel playing an important part in developing an art center for the community. Tell a businessman how his associates would regard him if he took the lead in funding a chair in business philosophy at his university. Ask your husband how he would feel if he agreed to your completing the degree you stopped working on to put him through school by working as a secretary.

These are the kinds of emotional rewards that the affluent, highly entertained people in our society prefer. Few people will be impressed by horsepower of a car, the number of students attending a college, or how many people are working for the Community Chest campaign. They are interested in exchanging their cooperation for good feelings about life and themselves. Thus, your attempts to gain commitment will go beyond facts and figures to the way people feel when they make use of the data you offer. Focus on the personal payoffs at this point and you will be far more successful in all kinds of situations with all of the personality patterns. A young man can say something like this:

> Alice, from what you tell me, I know that you love me as much as I love you. I understand how important it is to you to finish college with the others in your sorority, and I agree. That only makes sense. And I want us to be together now instead of waiting until graduation to get married. So I've come up with an idea that will give us what we both want. Would you like to hear it?
>
> I've found a summer job with a survey crew in the mountains. They pay all expenses and a good hourly wage, so I can save almost all I earn. We can get a student apartment next September and I've arranged my classes for the mornings only and I'll get a job for the afternoons and early evenings. This means that we could get married soon rather than waiting until graduation. How would that make you feel?

The winning of cooperation is not the only goal of your persuasion, of course. People cooperate to meet their needs and to solve problems, so a logical connection between cooperation and rewards must be maintained. In short, they want to be paid off. You must produce what you have promised, or else the cooperation will end.

Visual Imagery

Writing about television, Marshall McLuhan once commented that the medium is the message. His statement meant that the visual impact of television is so great that it obscures what is being said. Yet the impact of television is but a pale imitation of what the mind can produce when a person's imagination is turned loose.

A man or a woman can pick berries with a Cro-Magnon family, go through the depths of interstellar space in a starship, take part in the siege of Troy, make love to a celebrity, or become a millionaire, in the course of an hour. These are but a few of the mental images that a person can evoke for himself—or for someone else—when he knows what he is doing. You can use this ability to create visual images to help a person see what his reward can become when he does as you ask.

When conducting psychotherapy with students who were distressed about their feelings or behavior, I virtually always asked them to relax with me—using hypnosis if necessary to bring this about—and then I had them picture the kind of person they wanted to become. I had them tell me what their images were, whether they were free from stuttering, compulsive acts, deep-seated fears about sex that kept them from making love, or whatever. I had found that visualizing what one wanted to become was a powerful motivating factor in actually working to reach the goal. And each time the client came in, I had him close his eyes and conjure up that image of what he was working to become. Unfortunately, evoking such images is complicated by our limitations in communication.

Russell wrote that a large number of statements are bound to become garbled because they have to be formulated in the speaker's mind, then have to be filtered through his perceptual screen, and the process has to be reversed by the listener before it is acted upon. One of the clever signs of our times expresses our dilemma in conjuring up images for another person. My secretary had it on her desk to remind me to clarify my communication as much as possible. It said:

> I know that you think I understood what you said, but you
> didn't say what you thought you did, so I have no way of
> knowing what you want until you know what I thought you
> said.

It's probably incorrect to say that human beings are the
only species to use symbols to represent objects and concepts. It is a fact, however, that in many activities, symbols are not only people's medium of intellectual exchange,
the symbols frequently become more important than the
objects they represent. This is certainly true of the words
you can use to create the visual images that persuade. But
since words can represent such important rewards, they
must be well chosen and used wisely.

Keep the symbols and the presentation simple while
maintaining consistency with his level of education and
involvement. The academic dean at one of the colleges
where I taught expressed it this way. He said, only half in
jest:

> I need a month to prepare a fifteen-minute speech and I can
> get ready for an hour presentation in a few days. But if you
> want me to talk all day I'm ready now.

Keeping issues simple enough to involve his imagery
need not be difficult if you remember three concepts. They
are:

1. Use common, simple words and images.
2. Develop ideas logically.
3. Keep his participation active.

From the beginning of *Nice Guys Finish First*, I've tried
to teach you how to get into another person's frame of reference, because it is the most important thing you can do.
It is to your advantage to remain there without requiring
anyone else to learn your technical or philosophical vocab-
ulary while you are also asking him to cooperate with you.

Your persuasive power will be considerably increased if you learn to use his symbols instead.

Few people are impressed if you overwhelm them with a flood of concepts they cannot relate to their needs. They are more confused than impressed, and when people are confused, they have a strong tendency to find a safe place from which to weather the storm. They wait until you go away, wondering why you wanted to talk to them in the first place.

Use simple, ordinary words that have concrete meanings rather than abstract, involved phrases. Abstractions are often dry and juiceless. Concrete words are related to past experiences everyone has had. Use common words, make sure you are being understood, and apply them to the images he wants to have. You can say something like this:

> Just think how this could happen if you came to work with me. A year of commitment would put you and your wife on Maui at our midseason break with the rest of our salesmen of your caliber. Another year will see you in a new home on the lake, your kids in a good school district, and you enjoying the respect of the community. What kind of home would you and your wife prefer if money were not a condition?
>
> I can see you next summer, surfing in the blue Pacific with your cousins, flirting with the California girls, visiting the West Coast sights. What do you think it would be like for you?

It is important to make only one point at a time in a complex presentation. You want him to remain a participant, rather than to withdraw because everything has become a jumble he cannot sort out. Follow a logical presentation of information and accept his feedback about it to focus your request more accurately. The entire concept of programmed learning is based on a logical, step-by-step presentation of data.

A student is supplied with a subject and a device of some kind to present one point at a time. He has to learn specific information and use it to solve a single problem related to it. He is then told whether he was correct or not. If he was, he goes on to the next step in the program. If he was not, he is instructed to do the preceding step again until he does learn the right answer. In a sense, this is what your logical, step-by-step approach does for your prospective collaborator. To learn whether he has learned the "correct" answer you will have to check his feedback and ask questions that involve him in the discussion with you. His images and thoughts will tell you where to direct the conversation so you can have the most influence on his choices.

Painting Word Pictures

When you use images to help men and women formulate a better mental picture of how payoffs will personally benefit them, use ordinary incidents so as to make your points crystal clear. People think by forming mental images, especially when they plan for the future. They do this by isolating events from the past and combining them with their expectations in a new way. Obviously, the more familiar the images from the past, the more vivid the projection of future payoffs will be.

The difference between the familiar and the unknown can be understood for yourself by imagining that you are in your home or office and then comparing those feelings to the ones you have when finding your way around a distant city. You can also compare a familiar pub or restaurant to one where you are a stranger, entering for the first time without knowing how you will be received. You can enjoy the second situation, but there is no denying that the relationship tension will be greater. It will help to discuss ideas and events that are familiar to the person from whom you are asking commitment.

You should also relate the payoff to specific people, preferably individuals that he knows or knows about, since people are more interested in other people than in anything else. You will find that developing the rewards of cooperating as they relate to people is the most effective way of harnessing human imagination. You can take the most ordinary request imaginable and turn it into a vivid example by describing it through the experiences of other people.

Become the best storyteller that you can as you weave familiar, human, everyday experiences into stimulating appeals. In the business world, many executives reach a point where they are stymied because they have failed to develop their communication skills. As a result, one clever instructor did very well for himself teaching corporate managers and presidents how to communicate their ideas more effectively to the people whose commitment they need in order to remain winners.

I have rarely met a person who could not be captivated by a story that includes the advantages and rewards that others found by working together in important activities. Men and women are deeply interested in what has happened to others, even when they are turned off by facts. After all, Scheherazade saved her life for a thousand and one nights in *The Arabian Nights* by telling the sultan a different story each night. And no ideas ever gripped the imagination like those taught by Jesus Christ as he won the commitment of millions of people with his simple but profound parables about things that everyone else took for granted. His examples about the everyday experiences of men and women were so timeless that they have a dramatic impact on lives even yet, though the civilization that created them vanished two thousand years ago.

The people who have the greatest trouble painting word pictures to visualize rewards are usually Controllers and Comprehenders. In fact, they have about as much trouble in this area as Entertainers and Supporters have organizing appropriate facts and figures for presentations. Therefore, people above the horizontal line will need to improve their people-oriented skills more than those who have already learned how to use feelings easily.

Use plenty of rich, descriptive words, for these are the best instruments for conjuring the imagery that will convince others to accept your recommendation. Vivid images ignite the imagination in a way that facts or technical descriptions can never do, even to a Comprehender. Just don't become maudlin with people above the line. Use your communication skills to clarify rather than to obscure in the ways that politicians and intimidating salespeople do to make off with an occasional loaf while the dust is still settling. Describe events as they took place and as people would have witnessed them had they been there.

It is in organizing a presentation or a recommendation that Supporters and Entertainers need to take lessons from Comprehenders and Controllers. Since Supporters and Entertainers tend to be less organized, they need to think through some of the things they are going to say. Your request for help need not be memorized. In fact, it is best to let it remain spontaneous, although an outline memorized in advance will let you keep enough structure to remain logical and move toward a definite conclusion.

Overstreet taught that using a narrative is second best to actually putting a person in a situation, particularly if you use some tangible evidence to support your story. A narrative lets his imagination take over, which can be almost as pleasing and a lot less demanding than being there in person. A story, developed to fit what you have learned about his personality pattern and adapted to meet his needs, need not be any more canned than telling some friends about a soccer game or a wedding shower you attended.

What you succeed in getting a person to call forth in his mind through your words will most likely make the difference between his agreeing with you or refusing to cooperate. Not until he pictures himself enjoying the rewards and anticipating how he will feel when it happens will he be seriously interested. To sharpen his focus when using an anecdote, be sure to tell who the person was in the story, how he felt, what he did, and how the experience turned out for him. Make sure that he can see the actual person in his mind's eye and picture him enjoying the rewards of cooperating with you.

Finally, make the effort necessary to keep him a participant by including his feedback in your considerations. The actual words that you quote from others not only add color and drama to your request, they also make it much more credible. There are no more persuasive words you can use than an honest quote from a person who found his needs met by working with you. But in telling your stories, don't become so involved that you forget to tell him what you want him to do.

You would think that no one would be that foolish, to go through the tension and uncertainty of making a presentation only to fail to ask for help. Yet it happens all the time. One research study that followed more than a dozen salesmen for two weeks found an amazing problem. The researchers discovered that on more than 65 percent of their calls, the men did not ask their potential customers to buy their products! They quoted facts and figures, they displayed the samples and charts, and they related warmly. But they never took out their order pad and asked how many of the products the customer would like to order. Therefore their effectiveness was compromised.

Many men and women who want help do the same thing, and the people they talked to go away from them wondering what the purpose of the discussion was. People do this to avoid being rejected. If they don't ask, they aren't rejected. They don't win much in life, but they feel better about themselves for the time being. What you need to do is to realize that rejections, which will occur less and less frequently when you use the techniques taught here, are really rejections of concepts and ideas, not of you. If you separate people's refusals from you as an individual, they will be easier to accept. Work the percentages, but stack the odds in your favor by knowing what you are asking for, knowing when to ask for it, and making it easy for him to picture the benefits you are offering. If you have used the processes correctly, you have usually made a friend of him. At the very least this new relationship will leave the door open for a future time when you can ask for cooperation once more.

CHAPTER ELEVEN

Closing
the Issue

As your relationships mature into friendship, you will find yourself alternately assuring people of your support and concern, identifying needs and problems that can be met, and finally making the recommendations that make all of you winners. Real life does not move in a straight line the way a table of contents does. As my son said after he memorized a sales pitch for selling fire-alarm systems last year, "I know my lines, but my prospects don't seem to know theirs. They keep saying things I'm not prepared for."

Telephones ring and must be answered, secretaries demand signatures on important documents, kids skin their knees and need consolation and Band-Aids, and so on. New ideas come to mind out of sequence with your planned request, and they must be taken into account so as to maintain rapport.

The *Nice Guys Finish First* approach is effective, however, because it is not a canned presentation, but rather a general guide to how people can relate to each other supportively when they are willing to share the emotional, spiritual, and physical rewards that are basic to motivation. I *cannot* believe that any intelligent, normal person will give you the time of day if he perceives you to be manipulating him to reach your goals at his expense. If you are a parent, teacher, manager, or whatever, you can demand some degree of compliance for a while, but sooner or later it will catch up with you. Then you will lose as much as the people with whom you would not share the rewards of life.

When you are asking for commitment, if a person refuses, any attempt to force him into your circle of influence will only complicate matters. Do not try to overwhelm him with logic or facts as you go on the attack. But don't surrender, either. Remain his friend and continue to counsel him because of your expertise and your concern that he win the mutual rewards you both want from life. In this age, when you can no longer *demand* commitment, you can always help him see the ramifications of his decisions to cooperate or not. You can also help him understand the emotions that cause people to do things that are not in their best interests.

Unless you are a prison guard or a drill instructor in the Marine Corps, people are going to make up their own minds regardless of the pressures you use. But by following the techniques taught here, you will have a much better chance of persuading them than by merely tossing out answers in a take-it-or-leave-it manner.

Putting Pride in Perspective

Perhaps nothing causes as many interpersonal failures, at the moment of truth when you are asking for a choice, as pride. It can be your pride which somehow makes you afraid to lean forward, put your hand on his arm, and say, "I really need your help in this, Charles. Can I count on your help to make this program work?"

The pride that complicates issues may be his. It will block his acceptance if he feels that he is being manipulated and thus is losing his reward. In either case, there is a deep element of fear that is at work consciously or unconsciously when one's ego is being tested. Neither of you wants to be hurt, so you will often fail to do what is best for both of you to maintain as much pride as possible.

In the case of the person asking for help, self-esteem is a commonly seen but frequently pointless stumbling block that is bound up in our assumptions. With our John Wayne mystique, men especially have a confused picture of what masculinity really is. From childhood little boys are taught to stand on their own two feet, not to be a cry-baby, to do what they please, and to let the chips fall where they may. Little girls, on the other hand, are taught to negotiate and compromise to get their way. Perhaps the difference has more to do than we realize with the eight-year-longer life expectancy that women have over men.

I'm certainly not saying that self-esteem or pride is unimportant, for it is crucial to success and to good emotional health. After all, people have murdered, committed treason, and taken their own lives because they were unable to see themselves as important humans. Mental institutions and inner cities are filled with people who lost the battle for self-esteem.

If you hope to influence others regularly, you will have to keep your ego out of sight and allow others to sense the pride in accomplishment that will encourage them to cooperate.

At the moment of truth, rather than becoming defensive or moving from your comfort zone, answer the following questions.

1. How can I help this person overcome his fear?
2. How can I answer his objections so he can see the payoff?

3. How can I overcome the resistance and resentment
    caused by past adversary relationships?

When a person has expressed resentment with a company, a school, or your proposal, be willing to discuss his
feelings to help him gain relief by talking to you about
them. You can say:

> I hear you saying that you've had some unpleasant times here.
> Is that what you're telling me? It is too bad that some people
> reach places of authority who don't know how to treat other
> people. And I'd like to have you tell me what happened to
> you. That is, if you don't mind talking about it.

In most schools, families, companies, or whatever, most
people try to keep others quiet about unpleasant events, as
if talking about them would make things worse. Your being
accepting of his negative feelings may be the first time
in years that anyone has taken his feelings seriously, and
it will often melt his stubborn pride like the summer sun
on a block of ice. After he has gained some relief by discussing what has been troubling him, you can say:

> I certainly understand your feelings better now. I appreciate
> your honesty, as well. And I must admit that had I been
> treated like you have, I'd be furious also. And that's why
> people who know better should work more closely together.
> I'm sorry that it happened, but we're here now and we should
> work very hard to make life as good as we can. From what
> you've told me I'd expect you to be one of the first to want to
> end the old ways and make good things happen to all of us.
> May I tell you what I see happening among us as we help
> each other as best we can in this section?

Such a statement not only supports his ego and his perception of reality, it also closes with a challenge to help
you make things better for him, to improve the climate in
which mutual rewards can be found. By this time you will
be getting some messages which tell you whether he is
ready to cooperate or not. Keep your interpersonal, non-

verbal radar antennae tuned to pick up any signals that are coming back to you. Interpret them, and then act accordingly.

For example, a person in a discussion may relax abruptly, lean forward in his chair, smile, nod, or make an accepting gesture with his hands. He may ask commitment questions because he is visualizing himself with the payoff. Here are some of the commitment statements I have heard.

> It sounds like a pretty good idea to me.
> That just might do the job for us in Houston.
> How much of my time would you need?
> How could I tell if it was working for us?
> How much time would I have to spend in San Diego?
> When could we get started?
> I can't see how it would fail.
> How could I pay for it?

When you receive a message like this, stop relating, identifying, or rewarding, and ask for a commitment on the spot. He has convinced himself with facts and feelings, has visualized the reward you have spoken of, and is ready for you to make him an offer he shouldn't refuse. Any additional chatter or stories will likely turn him off, so get right to the issue, which is to confirm his acceptance of your offer. Of course you do not want to sit straight up with a look of surprise to ask, "Are you really going to do it?" as if he were the first person you ever persuaded to help you. Go ahead and act in his best interest.

Confirming His Decision

Few people are won to an important commitment in a single meeting or discussion. They need time to accept your personality pattern and to get past any lack of rapport caused by conflict of personalities. They need to trust you and to think through the ramifications of your offer, but in that case you will probably not have received the commitment statements or questions mentioned above. In addition, he fears making a mistake much more than you do at this point.

You at least know that you are honest and that he will share in the rewards of his cooperation, even if you are having some problems smoothing out the techniques. He's still worried about looking foolish in front of his friends and family. You can keep a gentle pressure on him, rather than simply leaving in surrender when he promises to think about the choices and call you next week. He rarely will, for you represent a new element in his list of priorities. You can require him to accept your offer or to make an issue of refusing to do so. This keeps both of you from losing by simple inertia or default. Use the technique given below only after you have seen signs that he is visualizing the rewards and is making commitment statements. To act too soon is to turn him off. To act too late will miss the tide of his emotions. When a person nods in agreement, smiles and leans forward as if reaching for something, or acknowledges that the cooperation would please him, make it easy for him to accept your offer and hard for him to reject it. You should:

> Expect
> Clarify
> Confirm

You *expect* that your friend is intelligent enough to see the benefits of acting in his own best interest.

You *clarify* his understanding and resolve any lingering doubts about the importance of acting now.

You *confirm* the value of the mutual payoff and his acceptance of them by using examples that are familiar and that are related to people with whom he can identify.

When you are convinced that the resolution you recommend is the one you would want for yourself were the situation reversed, your conviction can be seen in your non-verbal communication. When you know it's the right thing to do and he is agreeing with you, anticipate that his decision is going to be the same as yours and act accordingly.

Because you have paid your emotional dues to him while discovering his needs and problems, talked about resolutions and payoffs, and checked to see that he understands the advantages of cooperating and that the reward is appealing to him, you have earned the right to advise him. In his mind's eye he has seen what can happen and he assumes that you'll go ahead and ask for his commitment.

When you see the time has come to resolve the issue, he does also, for he has been a participant in the entire process. You believe that it is right and so does he. If you see some last-minute doubts that you had not anticipated, your concern will likely be communicated to him also. When these doubts have been resolved, go on and ask for his cooperation with the full confidence that he is intelligent and ambitious enough to cooperate with you. Say something like:

> When could you start work with me?
> Will you choose OSU or the U of O for your school?
> Do you want me to order your collection materials, or will you get them when you're downtown?
> Do you prefer a Wednesday class or a Friday class?

Every salesperson worth his salt uses this double minor point technique. It is very effective, for you are actually keeping him a participant in the choice. He need not feel that he has lost control, but only that he is making a choice, as he wants to. He is not being compelled to submit or to make an eternal choice, but to acquiesce or choose in a minor way with a supportive friend. His simple choice confirms that he has accepted.

Your Closing Move

If your friend has sent accepting signs and still refuses to respond to a simple either/or choice, he probably needs some minor doubt cleared up. Don't give up and go away. Slip back into the relating phase of the relationship, re-assure him that all is still well, find out what he needs as-surance about, and give it to him. He may even have a severe case of inertia, upon being asked to make a serious choice about his life, that must be overcome. It happens to all of us at times.

I agonized for six months before choosing my college and then chose on the basis of emotions, spent two months deciding on my last car, and a year deciding whether to leave college teaching. I also missed buying eighteen acres of orange groves in what is now downtown Phoenix because I wasn't sure there would be a payoff in time to pay for my college tuition. There wouldn't have been then, but I bloody well could have owned the college by now had I bought the land when I had the chance!

If you are typical, you know the feeling of uncertainty. You see the possible payoff, realize that you must act to get it, and then wonder why you should rock your canoe. After all, life is pretty good the way it is and there is always some-one after you to do something different. If only they would let you alone to concentrate on the football scores or the bowling league. You need time to put all the issues in per-spective, and your potential helper feels the same way. He probably wants the payoff, but he is momentarily catatonic with indecision. This is the time to:

> Review your request.
> Compare the rewards.
> Convince him with anecdotes.

The request can be reviewed in your own words by say-ing something like:

> To sum it all up, Don, I want a dynamic person like yourself putting his stamp on our Chicago operation. I'll give you free rein and back you up in your decisions. I'll also see that you get the credit you deserve and the help you need.

Comparing the rewards can include:

> I feel that your present outfit has peaked and, as you tell me, they have a long history of looking outside for general managers rather than promoting people who have earned the right to move up. They're complacent and I'm hungry for growth, as I believe you to be, so I'll work harder to help you become a divisional V-P before you're thirty-five. I don't see anyone doing that for you in your present company. Do you?

You could lead up to an anecdote that has a convincing ring by saying something like this.

> I don't want to have you make an off-the-cuff decision, but I'd like to know if you have any questions about my outfit? Anything we should discuss further?

A story or an example helps turn his questions or inertia into flesh-and-blood examples to convince him over the last hump.

> Perhaps you hesitate because you have made so many connections in your present company. You have friends there and people who know and respect you. I know just how you feel, for James Matson felt the same way when I persuaded him to come in with us. He felt that he was leaving part of his life behind. But just last week he dropped by my office for a chat. He said: "Boss, do you remember me telling you about Bill Addison with the Hudson Company? He was a real pistol there, but got aced out in a reorganization flurry. I think I've about got him convinced to take over my south side area. You've no objections, do you?"
>
> Of course I had none, for I want you fellows to run your own divisions. But my point is that Jim now has the authority to build the kind of operation he wants and to bring in the people he knows will get the job done for him. You can do the same when you have people you really feel strongly about, anyone who will help you get off to a good start for us.
>
> Would you find it more convenient starting in September or in October? I'd be able to spend some time with you the first of either month. Which is best for you?

The most successful negotiators are those who continue to find mutual rewards and who ask for cooperation despite the reluctance of people who are still making up their minds. The most persuasive people have learned that many people are so overloaded with requests and demands that they have been conditioned to say "No" to the first half dozen requests even when they see the advantage of cooperating.

When you learn to cope with reluctance to move by recognizing its source in uncertainty and inertia, you can continue to persuade until the automatic response has vanished in anticipation of the payoff. As a last resort, answer the last three questions, which still linger for most people who are having trouble accepting a sincere, profitable proposal.

> Will cooperation do what he says it will?
> Is this the best offer I'm going to get?
> Will the relationship between us last?

Continue to assure him of your support by telling him about other people who have become satisfied in a similar relationship. Give him facts and figures as needed, but refrain from overwhelming him with data. Pledge or contract in some way if that is needed. And finally, offer him, if at all feasible, a trial experience in which he need not burn his bridges. Show him how to get his feet wet without taking a life-or-death plunge. When he sees that the rewards are real, he'll be much more likely to give you the commitment you have been working for.

Then, when he has agreed to cooperate, show him that it is just the beginning of a mutually profitable relationship, not the end—and you will both receive many rewards in the months and years ahead. You will both be winners because of the supportive relationship.

Bibliography

Allport, G. W. *Pattern and Growth in Personality.* New York: Holt Rinehart & Winston, 1961.

Benson, H. B. *The Relaxation Response.* New York: William Morrow & Co., 1975.

Berne, E. *Games People Play.* New York: Collier, 1964.

Colm, H. *Existential Approach to Psychotherapy with Adults and Children.* New York: Grove, 1966.

Frankl, V. E. *Man's Search for Meaning.* New York: Simon and Schuster, 1958.

Frankl, V. E. *The Doctor and the Soul.* New York: Knopf, 1965.

Ginott, H. G. *Between Parent and Child.* New York: Macmillan, 1965.

Ginott, H. G. *Between Parent and Teenager.* New York: Macmillan, 1969.

Harris, Thomas A. *I'm OK, You're OK: A Practical Guide to Transactional Analysis.* New York: Harper & Row, 1969.

Lovaas, I. *Speaking of Behavior Modification.* New York: McGraw-Hill, 1974.

Maslow, A. H. *Toward a Psychology of Being.* New York: Van Nostrand Reinhold, 1968.

Rogers, C. R. *Man and the Science of Man.* Columbus: Merrill, 1968.

Rogers, C. R. *On Becoming a Person.* Boston: Houghton Mifflin, 1963.

Skinner, B. F. *About Behavior Modification.* New York: Knopf, 1976.

Skinner, B. F. *Beyond Freedom and Dignity.* New York: Bantam, 1973.

Wilson, L. A. *Managing Interpersonal Relationships.* Minneapolis: Wilson Learning Corporation, 1973.

Wilson, L. A. *Counselor Selling.* Minneapolis: Wilson Learning Corporation, 1972.